AS/A-Level

Religious Studies

Biblical Studies

Sarah K. Tyler

Philip Allan Updates
Market Place
Deddington
Oxfordshire
OX15 0SE

tel: 01869 338652
fax: 01869 337590
e-mail: sales@philipallan.co.uk
www.philipallan.co.uk

Cover illustration by John Spencer

Printed by Raithby, Lawrence & Co Ltd, Leicester

Contents

Introduction

About this guide

This question and answer guide has been written to provide you with a resource specifically aimed at helping you in your revision of AS and A2 material for the Biblical Studies papers in religious studies. It focuses on the common topics and issues across all the specifications. It is not exhaustive; some topics feature only on one board specification, and the constraints of space may not therefore allow for coverage of these here. However, the principles remain the same for all topics and you can learn how to apply these to the topics that are relevant to you.

There are 17 questions, all of which (except the synoptic question at the end) have two responses: one typically worth a C grade, the other an A grade. They are interspersed with examiner comments (preceded by the icon **e**), which will help you to identify their particular strengths and weaknesses. You should attempt the questions before looking at the answers and comments so that you can make a genuine comparison of your work with that of other students working at different levels of achievement. As you work through the questions, read the answers and absorb the principles outlined in the examiner comments. You will become increasingly familiar with the best approach to take and will find that your own answers improve with practice.

The aims of the AS and A2 qualifications

AS qualifications consist of three modules, which may include a coursework unit. Each module examines a specific discipline within religious studies and all specifications allow for a considerable diversity of options. You may be studying Old or New Testament in conjunction with Philosophy, Ethics, Church History or World Religions, so this subject is truly multidisciplinary. Furthermore, if you go on to A2 you will be required to demonstrate your awareness of how the different topics interlink and overlap. This is usually in the form of a synoptic unit, which is intended to give you the opportunity to *draw together your knowledge and understanding of the connections between different modules from across your full Advanced GCE programme of study*' (Edexcel). An example of a synoptic question is provided at the end of this book. This will guide you in some of the principles involved in writing a good answer that demonstrates your synoptic skills.

AS and A2 specifications in religious studies are designed to encourage you to do the following:
- **Develop an interest in and an enthusiasm for a rigorous study of religion.** Hopefully, your AS and A2 studies will be more than a means to an end for you. If you are interested in and enthusiastic about your academic studies you will do better in the exam, but you will take away from this subject something that I don't think

you can from many others. It has real 'value-added' features, exploring aspects of human life and existence that are of perennial interest to virtually everyone who thinks about the world and our place in it. A rigorous study is one that involves being critical in the best possible sense of the word: analysing and evaluating the views of others and substantiating your own. If you are not prepared to have your own assumptions challenged in a safe and supportive environment, then religious studies is not for you! You may not come away from it with your views changed, but you will have had the opportunity to evaluate them against those of scholars past and present, and those of your teachers and classmates.

- **Treat the subject as an academic discipline by developing knowledge and understanding appropriate to a specialist study of religion.** This should grow out of undertaking a rigorous study of religion. In the bad old days, people thought that RE, or scripture, was a safety net for those who were not very academic and who needed an easy option. Compulsory study of it in the earlier years at school did not always encourage students to see it as a valuable academic discipline to be pursued in the latter stages of their school career. That has all changed. AS and A2 students will be more than aware of the academic rigour necessary to do well in this subject, namely acquiring knowledge of the contribution of scholars to the subject and an awareness of what enormous diversity there is in the range of views offered. The discipline is dependent on the skills developed in many others: language, history, philosophical debate in its wider context, and literature. No one would study the works of Shakespeare without recognising it as an 'academic discipline', so why should this not also apply to religious literature? Disciplined scholars relate everything to the question, alluding to narrative and text rather than giving blow-by-blow accounts in ways that may or may not be relevant, and their responses are ordered, structured, and lead an argument to its logical conclusion.

- **Use an enquiring, critical and empathetic approach to the study of religion.** Enquiring scholars seek answers to questions of perennial importance, critically examining the arguments before deciding which they believe to be the most convincing or effective, but not rejecting the views of others without recognising that they are of great importance. Religious and ethical views make a difference to the way in which people lead their lives and scholars must therefore understand why they are held, even if they are not in agreement with them. We need to be aware of the historical, social and cultural influences on the way ideas have developed and of how the past leaves a legacy to the future. There are no 'right' conclusions to reach, but you will gain more credit for recognising the impossibility of definitiveness than for attempting to reach a dogmatic and non-empathetic conclusion.

Assessment objectives

Assessment objectives broadly fall into two categories:
AO1 — knowledge and understanding
AO2 — critical argument and justification of a point of view

More than 50% of assessment is concerned with the first objective, but you will not be able to move into the higher-grade bands if you do not demonstrate your ability to fulfil the requirements of AO2. You will show that you have fulfilled the objectives by the acquisition of knowledge and the deployment of skills. Hence, you need to acquire knowledge and understanding of:

- key concepts within the chosen areas of study and how they are expressed in texts, writings and practices
- the contribution of significant people, traditions and movements
- religious language and terminology
- major issues and questions arising
- the relationship between the areas of study and other specified aspects of human experience

You will also need to develop the following skills:

- recalling, selecting and deploying knowledge
- identifying, investigating and analysing questions and issues that arise
- using appropriate and correct language and terminology
- interpreting and evaluating relevant concepts
- communicating, using reasoned argument substantiated by evidence
- making connections between areas of study and other aspects of experience

As you move from AS to A2 you will be expected to demonstrate a wider range and depth of knowledge and understanding and a greater maturity of thought and expression, so the weighting of the objectives shifts as you move to A2. More marks are proportionally credited to AO2 than AO1.

Trigger words

The use of trigger words in questions enables you to identify the particular skills you are required to deploy. AO1 trigger words invite you to demonstrate your knowledge and understanding, while AO2 trigger words invite you to evaluate that knowledge. Trigger words you might expect to see in questions may include:

AO1 describe, examine, identify, outline, select, what, how, illustrate, for what reasons, give an account of, in what ways, analyse, clarify, compare and contrast, differentiate, distinguish between, define, examine, explain

AO2 comment on, consider, how far, to what extent, why, assess, discuss, consider critically, criticise, evaluate, interpret, justify

You need to be aware of the difference between 'give an account of' and 'consider critically'. To give an account you draw essentially on your knowledge, which you may *then* be required to evaluate through 'considering critically'. Considering critically, or assessing, or commenting on, involves drawing conclusions about the significance and value of what you have learned. There are certain phrases that you may find useful for this: 'This is important because', 'The most significant is...because', 'However...', 'On the other hand...', 'It is likely that...because', 'Therefore...', 'Nevertheless...', 'The implications of this are...'. As you work, keep asking yourself 'Why is this relevant to my answer?' and 'What are the implications of this view/issue?' Don't go onto automatic pilot, otherwise you will simply narrate facts or, worse, fiction!

Learning, revision and exam technique

As you prepare for your AS and A2 examinations there are stages that your teacher will directly help you with, and stages which you must be prepared to work on alone. In the end, teachers cannot go into the exam for you. While they can give you information and guide you in the best practice for utilising that information in the exam, you have to make sure you have learned the material and developed an effective examination technique.

Lessons

It is initially your teacher's responsibility to select the right information for your needs, but you need to take responsibility for the way you receive it and what you do with it after the class is over. So, develop good classroom habits. Ask questions about the material. Questions can help you to clarify what you have just heard, as well as clear up misunderstandings. Ask questions about the implications of the material the teacher is covering and about how it relates to other aspects of the specification. Your classes also give you the opportunity to practise the vital skill of evaluation. You will hear many views expressed which might be quite different from your own. You can — in an empathetic (non-confrontational) way — evaluate these: 'Am I right in thinking that you believe X to be right because of Y?' Be prepared in turn for your views to be evaluated by others, and to explain why you hold them: 'I think that Z is wrong because if you take Y into consideration, the conclusion cannot be X.'

Homework tasks

Because you have to write in the examination — indeed, the written word is the only vehicle you will have for assessment — you must use homework tasks as an essential tool for refining your written skills. One of the most useful things you should be doing for homework is practising past questions, as they will enable you to be totally at home with the way your board and specification require you to use the knowledge and under-standing you have gained. Your teacher can explain to you how he or she has marked your work in accordance with the principles laid down by the exam board so you can gain some insight into the way the system works. Every homework exercise is an opportunity to learn the topic you're working on, so don't just stick it in the back of your file when it has been marked!

Independent learning and consolidation

Even the best teachers are not going to cover absolutely everything in the class time available, although they will use that time to provide you with virtually everything you need to do well in the exam. However, it is the time you put in outside the classroom that will be truly decisive. You may read an article that no one else in your class has seen, watch a television programme, or simply go over your class notes one more time and, in so doing, finally understand a difficult area. There is no doubt that the top grades usually go to candidates who are prepared to do something extra, rather than simply attending classes and doing the work set.

Revision for the examination

It is never too early to start revising. From the moment the first topic has been completed in class you should be making concise revision notes, learning quotations and making essay plans. If you leave it until the exams are looming you will only have time to get the information into your short-term memory. You will feel far less able to deal with the unexpected, or to spend time in the exam ensuring that your written style is the best that you can offer on the day. Revision techniques do, and indeed should, vary. Everybody learns and remembers differently, so don't be led into thinking that you should be doing it exactly the same way as everybody else. Experiment with a range of strategies but make sure they are multisensory. Multisensory techniques literally involve using more than one sense. If you *read* your notes you are employing one sense only, but if you also rewrite them, read them out loud by working with another student or record them onto tape to listen to, then you are employing more than one sense. This will help to reinforce the work of the other senses, and your learning is therefore cumulative.

As you prepare for the examination, make sure that you are absolutely certain about key issues such as the day and time of the exam. You may think this is silly, but I have marked one exam paper on which a candidate wrote: 'Sorry about this, but I only just found out my exam was today.' This is not just a failure on the part of the school (if indeed she hadn't been told) but also a failure on her part not to make sure she did know the right day and time. Knowing dates well in advance enables you to make a revision plan, allocating specific tasks to each day as the exam approaches, so that your revision is never random or unplanned.

You also must be sure of what you will be required to do in the exam and how much time you have in which to do it. This is why you must practise exam questions under timed conditions. The best candidate may achieve a disappointing result because he or she didn't work to time, writing one or two long answers but resorting to a plan, notes, or a one-side-long offering for the others. If you have an hour and a half to answer two questions, that means 45 minutes per question, not an hour on one and half an hour on the other.

The examination

Remember, it's not over till the fat lady sings — so you don't have to be fatalistic about the exam. Keep calm and even if the questions are not the ones you hoped would come up, you can still use the material you have learned to answer relevantly the questions that are there. Do what you are asked and nothing else. Don't panic and leave early, but *think*. Read what you have written and check it for careless mistakes and misspellings. Ignore what everyone else is doing, even if they leave the room, faint or cry, and don't spend time in pointless postmortems after the exam.

What's done is done at that stage, and you need to have peace of mind to prepare for your next paper.

Remember

- **You don't have to be a genius.** If you follow the instructions, are conscientious, thorough and communicate with your teacher, you should do well.
- **It's not just down to being bright.** Remember the hare and the tortoise? The hare had natural advantages but did not build on them. The tortoise was naturally slower but he plugged away and eventually got to the winning post ahead of the hare. I have a student who is naturally exceptionally clever, but will he write an essay longer than a side and a half? He thinks being clever is *enough*, when persistence is the more reliable tool.
- **People are there to help you.** You need never feel alone in your quest for a good A-level grade. Every single member of staff at your school is on the same side as you, even if it doesn't always feel like it. But there are also other ways of getting help. Look out for revision courses and one-day or residential conferences, and encourage your teacher to attend exam board meetings. Everyone wants you to do well.

Tips as you approach your exam

What the examiner is looking for

- relevance
- coherence
- accuracy
- precision
- readable and well-presented answers
- evidence that you have taken an AS/A-level course — i.e. academic answers, not general knowledge

What the examiner is *not* looking for

- undergraduate-level answers
- perfection
- everything you know, whether or not it is directly relevant
- more than is realistic to expect of a sixth-form student

How you should approach the exam

- with confidence
- trusting your teacher
- knowing that you have done everything you can do
- knowing what to expect on the paper
- having had lots of practice

How you should approach revision

- simply
- in your own words
- by getting rid of unnecessary material

- with a pen in your hand
- actively
- in a multisensory manner

Revision killers
- reading through your file with music or the television on in the background
- working without a schedule
- working without reference to past questions

Acknowledgements
This book would not have been possible without the generous love and help of my premier division RS teacher, my unvanquished knight, who shares all this with me — and much more. With love, from your princess.

Sarah K. Tyler

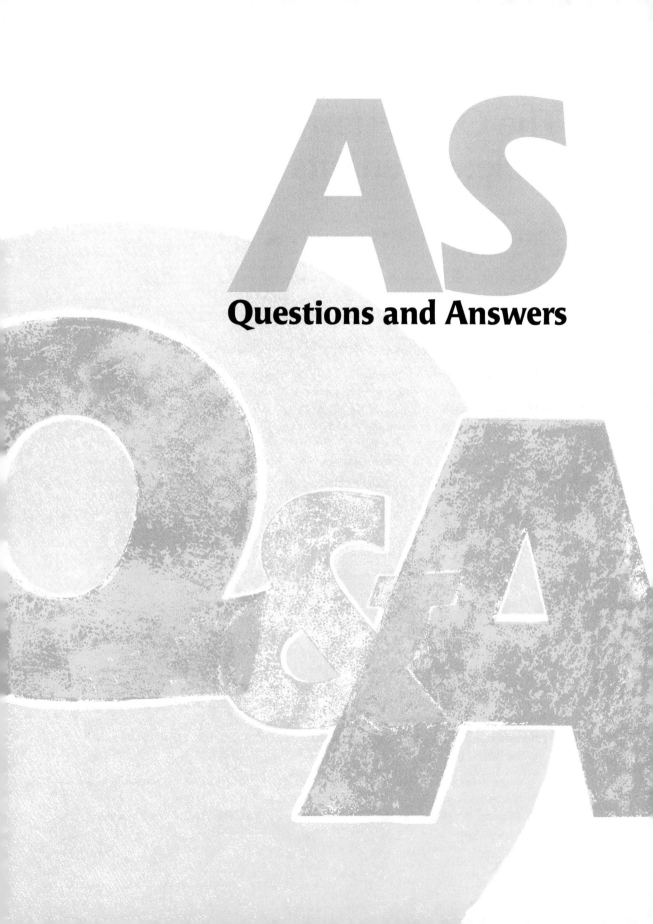

AS

Questions and Answers

The Old Testament/Jewish Bible: covenants

> **(a)** Explain the key features of three covenants made in the texts you have studied. (10 marks)
>
> **(b)** Discuss and analyse the extent to which the concept of covenant changes between Genesis 1 and Jeremiah 31. (10 marks)

A-grade answer to AS question 1

(a) A covenant is a binding agreement made between two parties that ties them to a relationship over a specified period of time and under specified circumstances. The dominant party usually sets out the terms of the covenant while a submissive party commits themselves to being obedient to those terms. In the Old Testament, covenants are made between man and God, but they are based on human covenants made between individuals and between nations. The whole of Israel's relationship with God is based on the concept of covenant, and John Hyatt writes: 'One of the most characteristic features of the Israelite religion was the belief that it rested upon a covenant between Yahweh and Israel, promising to worship him and obey his commandments.'

🄔 This is a promising start, with a relevantly used scholarly quotation, accurately remembered, and attributed to the right scholar. In Biblical Studies papers, the importance of this cannot be exaggerated if you are aiming for high grades. Use quotations wisely rather than indiscriminately, however. It is not the number of scholars you refer to that is important, but how helpful their contribution is to the argument of the essay.

Covenants are made with Abraham, at Sinai, and with David, and all three share similar features, although they are also distinctive. All covenants include promises, and to Abraham God promises land, blessing and descendants, promises that Von Rad observes 'run like a red line through the Patriarchal narratives'. At Sinai, God promises an exclusive relationship with his people and to go before them into Canaan and thereafter, and to David, God promises that there will always be a Davidic descendant on the throne in Jerusalem.

🄔 There is evidence here that the candidate is not just going to tell the stories but has recognised the specific instruction to 'explain the key features'. You cannot afford to drift off into general narrative, which will inevitably lead to lost opportunities to gain marks.

With promises comes commitment from both parties. God commits himself to a relationship with individuals and with a nation that excludes others. God chooses Abraham without any apparent reason, it is an act of his gracious favour, and in return Abraham is expected to put his faith in God, even in the face of enormous obstacles. When it appears that God's promise that he will have a child is to remain unfulfilled, he is encouraged by God to keep on believing, trusting God to break through in impossible circumstances (Abraham and Sarah are both way beyond their child-bearing years). Abraham shows 'a wonderful trait of absolute obedience when compared with a promise, the full importance of which he could scarcely surmise' (Otto Proksch) and ultimately his trust in God is vindicated with the birth of Isaac, despite the apparent lack of faith evident in his having a child with Hagar. At Sinai God assures the Israelites, 'If you obey my voice and keep my covenant, you shall be my treasured possession out of all peoples' (Exodus 19:5) — the commitment is on both sides of the agreement.

🄮 This candidate has skilfully blended use of scholarship with textual knowledge.

Special favour from God brings with it special responsibility, however, and all of those with whom God makes a covenant are called to recognise the obligations that it brings. The later Old Testament writers remind Israel of this covenant obligation: 'You only have I known of all the families of the earth; therefore I will punish you for all your iniquities' (Amos 3:2). When God calls Abraham to make a special commitment to him, Abraham can hardly imagine that he will later be called to sacrifice his son (Genesis 22). That he is not ultimately required to do so is not the point; it is his willingness to do so that matters. The descendants of David are offered special favour on the basis of David's relationship with God, but they are still called to obedience as individuals. Despite God's promises to David, the sins of his descendants cannot be overlooked and the exile to Babylon is eventually unavoidable.

🄮 The question asks for key features of three covenants and the candidate has presented these without ever falling into the trap of telling us things about the covenants, the individuals, or their circumstances which we don't need to know.

Finally, in each of these covenants an individual is called to have a significant influence on the generations that follow. The promises made to Abraham are personal to him, but he is told that 'by you all the families of the earth shall bless themselves' (Genesis 12:3). John Hyatt observes of Moses, 'The events of the exodus and Sinai require a great personality behind them'; the covenant made at Sinai is influential for many people, and the relationship that Moses shares with Yahweh is integral to its establishment. In the covenant made with David — 'Your house and your kingdom shall be made sure before me forever' — lie the roots of messianic hope that will influence generations long after the Davidic monarchy has ceased its reign in Jerusalem.

🄮 The candidate has established a strong formula for each paragraph: textual material, use of scholarship, and a careful drawing together of all the relevant strands.

(b) God makes a covenant at creation between man and woman and the whole created order and himself, entering into a relationship with them in which he will be the sustainer and provider, while man will be the steward, the tiller and keeper of creation. A key concept is established at this point — that of obedience. Man is told not to eat of the tree of the knowledge of good and evil, the only prohibition God makes, and the blessing of God is contingent upon man obeying that single command. When he fails to do so, God's protection is not entirely withdrawn: he makes clothes for the man and woman but removes them from the direct sphere of his influence by expelling them from the garden. In the same way, Israel is exiled to Assyria and to Babylon as a consequence of her disobedience. God's covenant love for his people is not withdrawn, but he cannot stand by and allow disobedience to go unpunished — covenants are rooted in the tacit agreement that each party will abide by their terms and on the understanding that they will be accountable for their violation.

> 🄴 This part of the question is potentially tricky, since there is a danger of repeating material or simply running out of inspiration. The candidate has not done this, and makes clear links between the material chosen and the demands of the question.

This does not change between Genesis 1 and Jeremiah 31. The covenant made at Sinai will stand for as long as Israel does not falter in her exclusive commitment to Yahweh, and it is only after her repeated apostasy that God's hand is forced. But even then, as Jeremiah promises, God already has plans for Israel's restoration. For the biblical writers, the exile is an opportunity, not the unremitting disaster that it appears to be. It is an opportunity for Israel to be reconciled with God again and to return to the honeymoon period of the wilderness wanderings. Hosea writes: 'And in that day, says the Lord, you will call me "My husband", and no longer will you call me "My Baal"...And I will make for you a covenant on that day with the beasts of the field...and I will betroth you to me in righteousness and in justice, in steadfast love, and mercy' (Hosea 2:16–19). God's overwhelming desire is for a covenant relationship with his people, and between creation and the return from exile this does not change. Punishment is for the purpose of restoration, not destruction.

> 🄴 Good textual knowledge is shown here, not only of the essential covenant passages but of material that demonstrates how themes are sustained throughout the Old Testament narrative.

All that Israel experiences through her covenant relationship with Yahweh, and which continues until she faces exile in Babylon, is dominated by the commitment that God has made to Israel and to the individuals he has chosen to receive his special favour. Against all the odds, Abraham sees the beginnings of the promise God has made, i.e. that he will be the father of generations, and despite the disobedience of his descendants to come, David is able to go to his grave knowing that there will always be a David on the throne in Jerusalem. God's commitment to his chosen people does not waver, and his promises in Jeremiah 31 reflect this. However, there is something new in the promises he makes here. The covenant is to be a 'new covenant', distinct in a special way from the covenant made with Israel's ancestors. God's promises will be written on the hearts of his people, so that their knowledge of God and their commitment to him will be intimate and deeply personal. Siegfried Herrmann suggests that Jeremiah 31 may have been written at a time when there was new hope that Jerusalem would be restored, but the promises contained within the passage do not depend on a physical return to Jerusalem, but rather on an awareness that Israel's covenant relationship with God remains for ever. It will be inclusive and rooted in the commitment that God has to every individual: '"They shall all know me, from the least of them to the greatest," says the Lord, "for I will forgive their iniquity, and remember their sin no more"' (Jeremiah 31:34). God's covenant promises endure for ever, and Jeremiah 31 offers new hope that they can stand, despite man's disobedience.

🄴 This strong candidate has reached a balanced conclusion and confirmed the impression that this is an A-grade response.

■ ■ ■

C-grade answer to AS question 1

(a) A covenant is a legal agreement between two parties and usually refers to the special relationship between God and the people of Israel. A covenant relationship was typically arranged by a stronger party and imposed on a weaker one, who would agree to the stronger one's terms. Many ancient alliances were made with covenants, and often conquerors would impose covenants on the peoples they had defeated. In the Bible, God is the stronger party and the people of Israel are the weaker. God initiates the covenant and the people respond.

🄴 It is good to start with a definition of an important term like 'covenant', but here the candidate spends far too long on unnecessary historical detail — the first sentence would have been enough.

The three covenants in the texts all have different key features. The first is the covenant with Adam and Eve, made in Genesis. It is a straightforward agreement made between God and Adam and Eve, in which God blesses them, gives them the Garden of Eden and tells them to 'be fruitful and increase in number' (Genesis 1:28). In turn, Adam and Eve agree not to eat from the fruit of the tree of the knowledge of good and evil. In fact, Adam and Eve are unable to keep their side of the covenant agreement.

🄴 This is a clear and straightforward explanation.

The covenant with Noah is made after the flood. As with Adam and Eve, God blesses Noah with the fruit of the earth and commands him to 'be fruitful and increase in number' (Genesis 9:1). God promises to care for Noah and never again to flood the earth. In turn, Noah promises not to eat meat with blood in it and to be held to account for the life of his fellow men. The covenant is marked by the sign of the rainbow.

🄴 As before, a clear account — the 'be fruitful' connection is a good observation.

The covenant with Abraham is considerably different. God promises Abraham his blessing, together with land and a multitude of descendants. In return, Abraham has to leave his homeland and agree to follow God. A covenant ceremony is held and animals are sacrificed. It is sealed in blood and with circumcision: 'You are to undergo circumcision, and it will be the sign of the covenant between me and you' (Genesis 17:10).

e This is correct, but rather vague. More could be said about Abraham's obligations and the fact that the covenant is to be passed on from generation to generation.

(b) The concept of covenant changes greatly between Genesis 1 and Jeremiah 31. In the first covenant, the agreement is only made between God and Adam and Eve and is a very simple one — it does not require them to shed blood or make sacrifices and God only gives them one rule to obey. By the time of Noah, the covenant is to apply not just to Noah but to his descendants as well. It requires greater faith and worship and Noah has to obey more complex rules. Moreover, in the covenant with Abraham, the agreement extends to a whole race of people and is sealed by a ceremony and in blood, and the people are 'marked out' by circumcision. God is involved in a more personal way.

e The candidate has the right idea here and makes some useful points. However, this part of the answer lacks detail — for instance, what are the more complex rules Noah has to obey? And in what sense is God 'involved in a more personal way' with Abraham? These are important issues that need to be addressed.

The covenant made with Moses (the 'Sinai Covenant') is not a new covenant, but extends the covenant with Abraham. It is made not just with Moses but with the whole nation, and the people of Israel are singled out as God's chosen people and are required to obey a number of specific laws. The scholar Drane points out that a covenant is an agreement in which people promise to fulfil God's commands and be loyal to him. Much later, the covenant with King David promises that God will establish the throne of David for ever, showing the everlasting nature of the relationship. However, by the time of Jeremiah, the nature of the relationship with God and his people is changing and Jeremiah speaks of a new covenant in the future, which will not be written on tablets of stone, but will be a personal commitment, written on people's hearts: 'I will put my law in their minds and write it on their hearts' (Jeremiah 31:33).

e The candidate makes some interesting comments here, although in a very generalised way. The essay is mostly narrative-based and the reference to Drane is not very helpful, since it tells us nothing we don't already know. To gain a top grade, more scholarly analysis and in-depth discussion is needed.

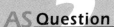

The Patriarchs

(a) Give an account of two episodes in which Abraham displays faith in God.   (10 marks)

(b) Outline one occasion when Abraham shows a lack of faith in God.   (4 marks)

(c) Assess the view that Abraham is a fictional figure rather than a historical character.   (6 marks)

A-grade answer to AS question 2

(a) Abraham is identifiable from the first as a man of faith and commitment to God. Otto Proksch observes that his response to God's call to leave his family, home and even his land shows 'a wonderful trait of absolute obedience when compared with a promise, the full importance of which he could scarcely surmise'. Without any assurance from the God who has called him to leave everything behind for a promise which seems beyond imagining, Abraham responds without questioning, much as Noah responded to the strange instructions to build the ark. The narrator indicates to the reader just how impressive is Abraham's faith, for we are told of two utterly conflicting elements in this new story. In Genesis 11:30 we are told that Abraham's wife, Sarah, is barren, and yet, in 12:3, God promises that he will be the father of nations. Only a miraculous act will reconcile this contradictory state of affairs, but it will be many years before this is accomplished. Without faith, Abraham's story could not even begin, let alone be fulfilled.

After his initial call Abraham is compelled to continue to be absolutely committed in faith, since the promises appear to be slow in being fulfilled. In Genesis 15 he asks God whether his slave Eliezer will be his heir, since no natural child seems to be forthcoming. Even in the face of such delay his faith holds firm and 'he believed the Lord and he reckoned it to him as righteousness' (Genesis 15:6).

Scholarship, narrative details and relevance to the question are immediately apparent here. An encouraging start to an answer that is not going to be pure narrative.

But the greatest challenge to Abraham's faith comes after the birth of his son. The reader is specifically told that God tests Abraham, calling him to 'Take your son, your only son Isaac, whom you love, and go to the land of Moriah, and offer him there as a burnt offering on one of the mountains that I shall show you' (Genesis 22:2). Claus Westermann notes that 'the words "your only son, whom you love" are directed at the audience of the narrative. They are intended to underline the harshness of God's

demand'. The level of Abraham's faith is again without question in this episode, as he takes Isaac, together with the materials for the sacrifice, and travels a 3-day journey to Moriah. Conversation between Abraham and Isaac is sparse, and the reader learns nothing of how Isaac feels, but the tension in the narratives is clear. Abraham's faith is sustained to the bitter end, and not until he raises the knife to kill his son does God intervene and provide the 'lamb for a burnt offering' (Genesis 22:7) as he had promised. The ultimate test of faith has been passed, leading God to confirm his promises to Abraham afresh. How the event affected Abraham and his son is of no interest to the narrator, but the commitment of faith that the Patriarch has demonstrated is of enormous significance.

> The real value of this answer is that the candidate has demonstrated textual knowledge without simply narrating. The candidate writes fluently and with a mature style, commenting on the narrative and demonstrating an understanding of it.

(b) A key episode in Abraham's life illustrates his lack of faith in God, however. Despite God's assurance to Abraham to 'Look toward heaven and count the stars, if you are about to count them… So shall your descendants be', Abraham accepts Sarah's suggestion that he have a child with Hagar, her maid. The situation classically reflects what happens when man's weak faith is unable to wait on God, but pursues an alternative human plan. Although the surrogacy is legal and culturally acceptable, it is not God's plan for the child of the promise. Inevitably, the situation is aggravated by natural, but unwelcome, emotional responses. Sarah is threatened and jealous, Hagar is helpless, and Abraham struggles to know how to respond. Abraham's lack of faith in God's promise, his assumption that human intervention is necessary for it to be brought to pass, does no justice to him or to his wife. However, as God was ready in the Garden of Eden to accommodate man's weakness, and provided garments for Adam and Eve to wear, so too does he accommodate Abraham's frailty and makes new promises to Ishmael. Although Ishmael is not the child of the promise, he too will be fruitful. But the promise to Abraham remains unchanged. He must continue to wait faithfully for the child of the covenant promise, and the episode brings from God a more specific time commitment: 'But my covenant I shall establish with Isaac, whom Sarah shall bear to you at this season next year' (Genesis 17:21).

> In this brief answer (appropriately so for the mark allocation) the candidate has demonstrated not only knowledge of a relevant episode but also how it relates to the rest of the narrative and to the relationships already established between the characters.

(c) The nature of the Patriarchal narratives has given rise to the question of whether Abraham had independent historical identity or whether he merely served a literary function. There is no evidence, archaeological or otherwise, to confirm or deny his existence outside the texts. However, A. Alt argues that a 'persuasive conclusion to this theory is that the formula "God of Name" indicates that the person who received the revelation was a historical personality'. In other words, when God addresses Moses at the burning bush as the 'God of Abraham...' Abraham must have been a historical figure for this to make any sense.

> e This is the tricky part of the question, which simply cannot be bluffed. This candidate is not bluffing — the response is rooted firmly in scholarly criticism.

However, some scholars have argued that the Genesis narratives have no factual worth. T. L. Thompson argues that 'the author had little interest in recording historical facts', and J. Van Seters claims that the 'traditions go back to the exile and reflect the experiences of that period'. Because the Genesis narratives were written so long after the events they describe, Bright proposes that 'all that can be said with assurance is that...the traditions...had by the earliest period of Israel's life reached normative form as part of a great epic narrative of Israel's origins'.

> e Good AO2 approach here — offering scholarly views for and against the argument proposed in the title.

However, Hermann argues that the 'three great figures of Abraham, Isaac and Jacob are hardly literary inventions to form a framework for the other relationships of affinity'. The characters have too much of a human dimension — Sarah is barren, she casts Hagar from her house, Abraham struggles to deal with the emotional dynamics of the surrogacy — but nevertheless, Bright observes: 'The Genesis narrative is painted in black and white, on a simple canvas, with no perspective in depth.' The narratives are not intended to be complex literary documents but simple, theologically profound accounts of Israel's origins through the redemptive acts of God. They are sacred history, which Von Rad defines as expressing 'everything that Israel had learned from her association with God down to the narrator's own time.'

> e While continuing to root the essay firmly in critical scholarship, the candidate also demonstrates knowledge of relevant textual material.

Although all we learn about the Patriarchs is completely dependent on the accounts of their experiences of God, A. Alt claims: 'we may not doubt that as recipients of revelation and founders of cults, the patriarchs were historical personalities'. The literary picture of Abraham is not idealised as is that of David, which presumably it would have been were it not rooted at some level in history. Nevertheless, the importance of the narrative remains, irrespective of historicity, and finds its fulfilment in God's revelation at Sinai.

> e A neat conclusion, drawing together all the evidence, confirms this response as a very secure A grade.

■ ■ ■

C-grade answer to AS question 2

(a) Abraham has to display faith in God when he is called to leave his land and his home.

For no apparent reason, he receives a call from God to make a journey to a new land, leaving behind his home, his family and his land. God makes a promise when he calls him to do this, but there is no reason why Abraham should respond unless motivated by faith alone. His nomadic lifestyle enables him to take with him his servants, flocks and herds, but nevertheless it is a not inconsiderable upheaval for a man who may not previously have worshipped Yahweh.

> This has started with the same episodes as the previous answer, but immediately we see that the presentation is far less sophisticated, with no scholarly support and a more limited approach to the text.

Abraham responds to God's promise to make him a great nation, but there is further reason for Abraham to demonstrate great faith here — his wife is barren. We are told this because we will then be sure that only a great miracle will be sufficient to fulfil God's promise. This is a feature that is often used in the Bible, for example, Hannah. However, this does not deter Abraham, who responds immediately to God's commands, even though there is no obvious way in which the promise will be fulfilled. Otto Proksch calls this 'a wonderful trait of obedience'.

> This is a typical way in which middle-range candidates use scholarship — brief, half-remembered quotations that only tell part of the story. The allusion to Hannah is also rather random.

Another episode which demands great faith from Abraham is when God commands him to sacrifice Isaac. This is hugely ironic, since Isaac is the child that God promised to Abraham and for whose birth he waited for many years. However, once again, Abraham does not hesitate but immediately begins the journey with Isaac. He is faithful right up to the last moment, and only when he is about to plunge the knife into Isaac does God intervene and provide an alternative sacrifice. Abraham has passed the greatest test to his faith that he could have endured.

> Overall, this part of the question has not been dealt with in much depth.

(b) Abraham shows lack of faith in God, however, on several occasions. One of these is when he is in Egypt and is faced with the prospect of Pharaoh taking Sarah, Abraham's wife, into his harem. This story is told twice of Abraham and once of Isaac and his wife, Rachel, so it is clearly a popular device for the narrators to show the threat that may have hung over the promise God had made. The story is sometimes referred to as 'The ancestress in danger'. Abraham should have trusted God to look after him and Sarah, but instead he tells Pharaoh that Sarah is his sister, assuming that Pharaoh will not kill Abraham in order to possess her if that is the case.

However, God does protect Sarah in the harem and the other women there speak highly of her. At night, God sends plagues on Pharaoh's house because of Sarah's captivity and Pharaoh realises that they are due to the visitors. He is angry that Abraham deceived him, which showed a lack of trust in Pharaoh's integrity. He immediately lets Abraham and Sarah go. It is strange that this story is told again of Abraham and Sarah. Presumably it was the same story repeated in a different context.

> e Credit is due to this candidate for using a less obvious episode than the one used in the previous answer. The discussion here is a little disjointed, but acceptable.

(c) Because we know very little about the circumstances of the Patriarchs and about their individual lives other than what we read in Genesis, it is not surprising that scholars have suggested that Abraham may not have been a real character. Some archaeological findings, however, may have contributed to our knowledge of the Patriarchs. Discoveries made at Mari and Nuzi, for example, tell us something about the customs of the time, which the Patriarchs also seemed to follow.

> e This answer is clearly simpler in approach than the previous one, but the angle taken is legitimate.

For example, the Nuzi discoveries show that a childless woman could allow her husband to have a child with her slave girl, and the child would then belong to the woman and her husband. This is what happens with Sarah, Hagar and Abraham. Sarah was Abraham's half-sister and we also know that families could intermarry more freely in those times.

However, the historical accuracy of the Old Testament accounts is not entirely clear. The narratives are sagas, accounts of events that cannot be precisely dated or rooted firmly in history, but that represent the beginnings of Israel as a religious nation. Also, archaeological findings only tell us things that are quite general — for example, they do not provide us with names of any of the Patriarchs.

The material was probably handed down orally too, and although this was a more common method in those days, it means we cannot pin-point its origin precisely. However, scholars such as Bright have suggested that the Patriarchal stories are nevertheless deeply rooted in history, although it is religious, or salvation, history. There is no reason to dismiss the reality of Abraham.

> e Overall, this candidate has made a good attempt at making general observations about why the narratives should be considered to be historically reliable. However, more specific reference to scholarly debates, as illustrated in the earlier answer, would be needed to raise the grade above a C.

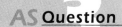
The Monarchy

> **(a)** For what reasons do the Hebrews ask Samuel to appoint a king? (10 marks)
>
> **(b)** What are the warnings Samuel gives against having a king? (4 marks)
>
> **(c)** To what extent do these warnings come true in the reign of Saul? (6 marks)

A-grade answer to AS question 3

(a) 'You are old and your sons do not follow in your ways; appoint for us a king to govern us, like other nations' (1 Samuel 8:5). The request for a king is made to Samuel for many reasons, not least for the two specifically outlined in 1 Samuel 8:5. Samuel, like Eli, cannot look forward to his sons taking over after him, since they have proved themselves unsuitable for leadership, and the time is ripe for Israel, hitherto a shifting tribal confederacy, to become a united nation. However, the reasons for the request run deeper than this. The Philistine threat that faces Israel at this point in her history is a real one; the Philistines have the monopoly on iron smelting, and a large, powerful and regular army. After years of gradual infiltration and settlement in Canaan, Israel must now make herself like the other nations if she is to win respect as a nation with real military, political and economic power.

> **e** The circumstances of the request for a king are placed within the cultural setting that provides a context for the whole essay.

Israel has survived thus far as a tribal confederacy on the basis of her old theocratic, covenant relationship. The tribes remain independent of one another, joining together only for religious purposes, and when military danger threatens a tribe, they are reliant on their own defensive resources and on the leadership of a judge. Ralbag observes that a 'king would be able to mobilize the whole people behind him whereas before only those immediately attacked had resisted and the rest of the tribes had refrained from helping them'. Judges were charismatic leaders, anointed by Yahweh to meet a particular crisis. They were temporary leaders whose role was complete once the crisis was passed, and they served only to unite Israel's military resources during that time. As such, they did not bring long-term military status to Israel, but rather they fulfilled a role in the Deuteronomistic Cycle.

e As long as they are not overused, diagrams are perfectly acceptable.

This cycle leaves Israel vulnerable each time she falls into a pattern of disobedience, since there is no permanent leader to represent her as a strong nation to her enemies, and the lack of a king renders Israel essentially different from the surrounding pagan nations. A new stage in Israel's history demands new leadership, and despite Samuel's warnings, Israel's elders insist that the time is ripe for Israel to acquire the status that will identify her with the nations amongst which she can trade and with which she will inevitably engage in military conflict.

e All the essential information is here, without falling back on story-telling.

(b) Samuel speaks as the mouthpiece for the Deuteronomistic editors in the warnings he utters about the monarchy. The editors are clear that the monarchy has been the reason for Israel's exile, as the kings lead the people into apostasy and further from their covenant relationship with God. Samuel sees the request as a violation of the theocratic nature of Israel's society. Since the Israelites entered Canaan, God has been their king, and the appointment of a human monarch will seriously undermine their commitment to their divine ruler. Already easily tempted by apostasy, Israel's closer identification with the pagan nations that surround her will lead her further into worship of pagan gods. Samuel is also influenced by personal factors. The rejection of his sons must have been bitterly ironic after Samuel himself had been appointed as the successor to Eli, whose own sons had failed to prove themselves worthy successors to the priesthood. Yahweh reassures Samuel that the people have not rejected him, but God himself, and sends him back to the people with a solemn warning of what they are to expect. David Gunn notes that the 'reader is warned that the forthcoming experiment in kingship is unlikely to be successful'.

e What is impressive about this answer is the inclusion of the essential information without resort to a list of narrative points. The style is fluent and scholarly even when textual material is being outlined.

(c) Samuel's warnings do not, however, reflect the reign of Saul. Rather, his predictions of a king who will 'take your sons and appoint them to his chariots...your daughters to be perfumers and cooks and bakers...your male and female slaves...one tenth of your flocks...' (1 Samuel 8:11f) reflect more accurately the conditions under which Israel laboured during the reign of Solomon. Nevertheless, if Samuel was convinced that the monarchy was to be a failure, the reign of Saul as it is related in 1 Samuel is certainly presented in a dismal light.

Saul's relationship with Samuel is ambivalent. It is not entirely clear what Saul does to offend Samuel so deeply, and Hermann observes that a 'personal conflict between Saul and Samuel is quite conceivable as another unwelcome element in this situation'. Nevertheless, Saul is clearly presented as being disobedient to the letter of Samuel's instructions on two occasions, when he offers the sacrifice before the battle (1 Samuel 13), failing to wait for Samuel to arrive to offer it himself, and when he refrains from carrying out the full sacred ban on the Amalekites (1 Samuel 15), saving King Agag and the best of the livestock. Whatever Saul's motives for so doing, as far as Samuel and Yahweh are concerned, his disobedience renders him unfit to be the founder of a dynasty, and already God has sought out his successor. Nevertheless: 'The question revolves itself around the motives of Samuel and God. Does the real cause of his rejection lie in the attitude of God towards him or perhaps something he represents?' (John Hyatt).

Saul fulfils the functions that Israel had demanded of her king. He leads Israel in successful campaigns against the Philistines, taking on a role that was inevitably going to be difficult in a transitional stage. Israel is still essentially a tribal confederacy under Saul, with no sophisticated court as later emerged under David and his descendants. Saul needs the link with Samuel, the last of the old order, to survive, and when he fails to maintain Samuel's loyalty, his own weakness of character prevails. As David becomes prominent, Saul's jealousy affects his ability to make wise decisions and he becomes an increasingly sorry figure.

With David, the monarchy effectively starts again, and the Deuteronomistic editors offer him their unqualified support. Nonetheless, the monarchy itself is doomed and from the division of the kingdom under Solomon, it is clear that its days are numbered.

e In this substantial answer the candidate has continued to combine all the skills necessary for a strong A-grade answer.

■ ■ ■

C-grade answer to AS question 3

(a) The people of Israel come to Samuel to ask for a king because they need a king to lead them into battle against their enemies. Without a king they are at a military disadvantage because they do not have a figurehead to lead them into war and to give them the respect that the other nations have. The Israelites were facing enormous conflict from the Philistines at the time of Samuel, because the Philistines had not only a king but a very strong military force and the monopoly on iron smelting. With these advantages they could push the Israelites into a very tight corner, although it is interesting to note that Samuel had in fact already led them into battle against the Philistines in chapter seven, and won.

e This is all a bit waffly. The point is made and there seems to be an attempt at evaluation at the end of the paragraph — identifying an inconsistency, perhaps — but we could do with knowing more about the background and circumstances of the Israelites at this point in their history.

Israel was in a difficult position because she had colonised the land of Canaan, but because she was still essentially a tribal grouping and not a nation, she did not have the status she needed to confront the other nations in the region. The tribes did not form a permanent army and they relied on temporary armies whenever there was some kind of military threat. With a king, Israel could have a permanent military force which would be on hand for surprise attacks and to deter enemies.

Judges governed Israel before the monarchy was established, and while this system had apparently been successful, something more permanent was now needed. A judge only governed temporarily but a king would be there all the time and would represent a stable nation with political identity. If Israel was more like the other nations it would be better able to maintain a strong presence in Canaan.

> ⓔ All the basic information is here, but there is no scholarship and no discussion of the characteristics of the Deuteronomistic History, which are so influential on these narratives. No textual quotations appear either.

(b) Samuel warns the people that their request for a king is wrong for a number of reasons. Firstly, he believes that they are rejecting God. Israel had been ruled by God since their earliest times and had had no need for a king. This is because she was a theocracy — ruled by God. Having a king would mean a change of status in this respect.

Secondly, having a king would make the nation like her surrounding pagan neighbours. The Israelites specifically ask Samuel for a king to 'govern us like the nations', suggesting that they are no longer satisfied with being a distinctive nation. The covenant relationship they have with God is intended to make them different from the other nations, and in asking to be like these other nations they are betraying the specialness God intends them to have.

Samuel is personally unhappy that he and his sons are being rejected from their position. Samuel would have expected his sons to take over as judges after him, but they are evil.

Samuel also warns the people that having a king will mean changes in their lives that they probably have not considered. He tells them that the king will take their flocks and herds and put them to his own use, and will take their children to be his servants. The cost to life and liberty will be high.

> ⓔ This is very straightforward AO1 material, without a glimmer of style or value-added quality — no scholarship and no direct quotations. It isn't wrong so it would gain credit, but not at the highest level.

(c) The reign of Saul is a personal disaster for Saul but does not particularly affect the people of Israel, so Samuel's warnings do not come true in the way that he says. Saul does not take the people's livelihoods for himself, or cost the nation money to keep the court in the way that Solomon does. However, in more subtle ways, the warnings may have come true.

> ⓔ This is rather promising. The candidate will now need to develop an argument from the text about the 'subtle ways' in which Samuel's warnings are fulfilled.

Samuel was concerned about the loss of covenant identity in having a king and warned the people that the only basis on which God could bless the monarchy would be if the king was totally obedient. Saul is not, and because of that he loses the hope of a dynasty after him. Saul taints the kingship, so the reign of the first king is seen as a great disappointment for the writers of Samuel. Only when David becomes king do they see some hope, but even then David's son, Solomon, is a failure because he worships other gods, and so, ultimately, all that Samuel warns about happens.

Samuel's warning about disobedience is important for understanding why Saul is a failure. He doesn't seem to do anything particularly wrong, but if the king is expected to be absolutely obedient to the last word of God's commands then he fails — he does not wait for Samuel to come to offer the sacrifice before the battle, and he fails to carry out the sacred ban on the Amalekites. This is all a warning for future kings — unless they are obedient, the monarchy will fail. Saul needs the support of Samuel, which he loses, and after that there is little he can do. John Drane points out that Samuel is forced to go against the tribal ideals of his people and that was why he fails.

e Quite a thoughtful response, but no direct quotation from the text, and no development of scholarly points. The reference to Drane is something of an afterthought. Compare this essay with the previous one, in which the candidate develops an argument, considering the strengths of Saul as well as his weaknesses.

The New Testament: the Birth Narratives

> **(a)** Give an account of the conversation between Mary and the Angel Gabriel. (6 marks)
>
> **(b)** Describe the roles played by (i) Zechariah and (ii) Joseph in the Birth Narratives. (8 marks)
>
> **(c)** To what extent do the Birth Narratives show the fulfilment of prophecy? (6 marks)

A-grade answer to AS question 4

(a) Luke portrays the birth and infancy narratives through the eyes of Mary, possibly prefiguring the interest he has in women's roles in Jesus's ministry. The annunciation to Mary is a surprise to her, and the reader is given no reason to assume that she expected any such visitation. She is described as betrothed to Joseph, a Davidic descendant, but otherwise we know nothing of her circumstances. Gabriel greets her with the unusual salutation 'Hail, O favoured one, the Lord is with you!' (Luke 1:27) which unsurprisingly puzzles her. Gabriel tells her that having found favour with God she is now to bear a son whose name will be Jesus. The angel prophesies Jesus's future roles: the Son of the Most High; Davidic king; ruler over the house of Jacob and of an eternal kingdom.

> **e** All that this part of the question requires is knowledge of the narrative, but this candidate has presented it with such style that we are left in no doubt that its implications as well as its content are understood.

Mary wonders how this is to be accomplished, although her question to Gabriel is not interpreted as an expression of doubt as Zechariah's earlier question was. Gabriel tells her that it will be by the power of the Holy Spirit that she will conceive a child 'called holy'. It is clear from the conversation that the child will be nothing less than the Son of God. Luke parallels the births of Jesus and John the Baptist, and Gabriel tells Mary that her own pregnancy is not the only miracle that God has performed. Her barren kinswoman, Elizabeth, has also conceived and is 6 months pregnant. Mary willingly accepts all that Gabriel has told her, as she thoughtfully considers all that happens throughout the ensuing narrative.

> **e** The conversation has been carefully outlined so nothing is missing, and the candidate has managed to allude to the significance it has for the narrative as a whole.

(b) Zechariah and Joseph represent old, pious Judaism, but interestingly, their roles are perhaps less positive than those of Mary and Elizabeth. Zechariah is a priest in the temple, carrying out the rare privilege of burning incense, an honour likely only to come to him once in his lifetime. He is evidently devout and Gabriel's words suggest that he and Elizabeth, like Abraham and Sarah, have been waiting many years for God to answer their prayers for a child. However, while Abraham believed God's words and 'it was reckoned to him as righteousness' (Genesis 15:6), Zechariah's immediate response is one of doubt, and he is told that he will remain dumb until his son his born. Only then does Zechariah demonstrate the faith that such a miracle demands, writing 'His name is John' before the eyes of his amazed neighbours, and his speech returns. Zechariah has been compelled to lay aside his presumptions about how God works as Abraham was also compelled, and once he has done so he is able to praise God and be filled with the spirit of prophecy. In his song, he anticipates the role his son will play and, by implication, the role of Jesus too. John will be the prophet of the Most High, preparing the way for the Lord who is to come after him. Zechariah recognises that both John and Jesus are to share in the fulfilment of God's plans and purposes for his people, and despite his earlier doubts, he is now able to accept the part he has had to play in the unfolding of the next era in salvation history.

> **e** The candidate has obeyed the instructions and kept the material about Zechariah and Joseph separate. Although this is another essentially fact-based answer, the sense of understanding and implicit analysis raises it to the top level. A technical term such as 'salvation history' ought to be explained, however.

Joseph's role is significantly less prominent in Luke's account than it is in Matthew's. He only serves to fulfil the role of the Davidic descendant with whom the Messiah must be associated. We hear nothing of his response to Mary's pregnancy or to the birth of Jesus, the shepherds' visit, or the prophecies of Simeon and Anna in the temple. He is a silent presence, who functions as the means for Jesus's birth in Bethlehem, and as a consort to Mary. He takes no initiative and makes no observations. Only through Mary's words do we learn by association that he too was worried when the 12-year-old Jesus was left behind in Jerusalem at the Passover, on which occasion Joseph is referred to as Jesus's father (Luke 2:48). He is associated with Mary too when Luke reports that Jesus grew up obedient to his parents (Luke 2:21). Whilst Joseph must have known about the circumstances of Mary's miraculous pregnancy, Luke, unlike Matthew, has no need to describe his reaction or his response. His role as the Davidic link alone is sufficient.

> **e** The candidate has managed to make something out of very little here. Joseph has a minor role in the Lucan account, and this in itself is interpreted as being significant.

(c) Morna Hooker observes that although there are no actual Old Testament quotations in the Lucan Birth Narratives, the two chapters are a 'pastiche of Old Testament allusions' and are written in an Old Testament style. She argues that this is part of Luke's strategy to signal to his readers that the story he is telling is the 'next, and crucial, chapter in the story of salvation'. The Birth Narratives function as the means by which the reader learns how prophecy is to be fulfilled in the coming of Jesus. God's promises to Abraham are in focus in the births of both Jesus and John, and Mary and Zechariah serve as the prophetic voices in the narratives.

> It is good to see accurate use of a reliable scholarly source, applied to illuminate a genuine scholarly point, rather than 'Marshall says that Jesus was born in Bethlehem' or something of that feeble nature.

John the Baptist is presented as the returned Elijah, the fulfilment of Malachi 4:5, who will come before the Messiah to prepare God's people for repentance and salvation. John himself strikes a remarkably Old Testament figure, possibly a Nazarite like Samuel, and as the prophet of the Most High he stands at the end of a long line of God's prophetic men who have prepared for this moment.

God's promises to both Abraham and David are fulfilled in the birth of Jesus. In Genesis 12:5 God assures Abraham that he will be the father of a multitude, generations that lie centuries after Abraham's own lifetime. Zechariah sings that God has now remembered 'his holy covenant, the oath which he swore to our father Abraham' (Luke 1:72–73), and Mary, too, praises God for how he has 'helped his servant Israel ...as he spoke to our fathers, to Abraham and to his posterity for ever' (Luke 1:54–55). In Jesus, too, the promise that David would always have a descendant on the throne is fulfilled. He is born in Bethlehem, as prophesied in Micah 5:2, and both Gabriel and Zechariah refer to the house and throne of David over which Jesus will rule.

> Good Old Testament knowledge is needed for this question, which this candidate has clearly demonstrated.

When Jesus is brought to the temple as a baby, Malachi 3:1 — 'The Lord whom you seek is suddenly come to his temple' — is fulfilled, and Simeon's words echo Isaiah 42:6 — 'I have given you as a covenant to the people, a light to the nations'. Both Anna and Simeon, representatives of faithful Jews waiting patiently for God's revelation, clearly understand that Jesus is the expected Messiah. The Birth Narratives serve effectively, therefore, to demonstrate to their readers that the salvation that comes through Jesus is the continuation of the story of how God saved his people in the past.

> This would be another clear A-grade answer.

■ ■ ■

C-grade answer to AS question 4

(a) Luke reports that in the sixth month the Angel Gabriel was sent to Nazareth with a message for Mary that she was to bear the Son of God. Mary is described as a virgin betrothed (engaged) to Joseph who is of the line of David. The angel says, 'Hail, O favoured one' which means that Mary is blessed by God, although she does not understand why this is so. She is afraid, but Gabriel tells her not to be afraid and that she should call the child she will bear Jesus. Gabriel prophesies that Mary's child will be the Son of the Most High, reigning over the throne of David for ever. He is to be the Messiah. When Mary asks how this is to be so, Gabriel tells her that it is through the power of the Holy Spirit. He also tells her that Elizabeth is pregnant with John the Baptist.

> There is something about this response which smacks of verbatim Sunday School accounts. It is half the length of the previous candidate's answer and lacks any sense that the narrative has been made the candidate's own.

(b) Zechariah is the father of John the Baptist and he and Elizabeth are parallel characters to Mary and Joseph, just as Jesus and John are paralleled in the stories. Like many biblical characters, he and Elizabeth have been unable to have any children, but one day when he is burning incense in the temple an angel tells him that their prayers have been heard and they will have a son. However, Zechariah, unlike Mary, is disbelieving and asks for a sign. Although he is a pious, believing Jew, he is not able to accept the miracle until it actually happens. The angel tells him that he will be dumb until John's birth and only then will he be able to speak again.

When John is born, Zechariah shows that he is a man of faith after all, because he confirms that his son is to be called John. This is unusual, because there was no one in the family by that name, but Zechariah writes on a tablet 'His name is John' and this shows that he has accepted everything that the angel told him. His prophecy (the Benedictus) speaks of all that John is to do, going before the Messiah to prepare his ways. Zechariah stands on the edge of the old and the new ages.

Joseph plays less of a role in the narratives than Zechariah. He doesn't speak and, in fact, Mary speaks for him when they find Jesus in the temple when he is 12 years old. However, this role is that of the Davidic descendant which Jesus needs to be the Messiah. Joseph takes Mary to Bethlehem where Jesus is to be born according to the Old Testament because he is from the Davidic line and the town of David. Along with Mary, Joseph takes Jesus to be dedicated in the temple and they go to the Passover in Jerusalem when Jesus is a boy, so Joseph, like Zechariah, is a pious, law-abiding Jew.

> In response to these essentially fact-based questions there is not an awful lot you can do except accurately relate the narrative. The best marks are gained by the candidate who has the style and flair to do so in a way that also demonstrates understanding. The answer of the previous candidate is clearly more effective in this regard.

(c) The Birth Narrative is entirely concerned with fulfilment of prophecy and Luke shows that he is interested in showing that the births of Jesus and John are the fulfilment of the promises made by God in the Old Testament. The whole narrative has an Old Testament flavour, beginning with the granting of a son to barren parents who are very similar to Sarah and Abraham. John fulfils the promise that Elijah will return before the coming of the Messiah, and we are told that he will 'go before him in the spirit and power of Elijah'. By this we know that the Messianic Age has begun — a new era in salvation history.

🄴 As mentioned before, a technical term such as 'salvation history' really ought to be explained.

Jesus fulfils the promise that was made to David that he would always have a descendant on the throne in Jerusalem. Even when the monarchy came to an end this hope continued, and now Jesus is to be the king who will reign for ever. Mary also says in the Magnificat that Jesus's birth is the fulfilment of promises made to 'Abraham and his descendants forever'. In Genesis 12 God promises Abraham that he will be a blessing to all nations, and this is fulfilled in the coming of Jesus. Jesus is descended from Abraham and from David, so fulfilling the promises made to both. Zechariah's song confirms this.

Jesus's being born in Bethlehem fulfils the prophecy of Micah 5:2, and the use of shepherds echoes the many Old Testament references to God being a shepherd over his people and the promise in Ezekiel 34 of a Davidic shepherd who will rule over Israel.

🄴 Like the answers to (a) and (b), this is inconclusive. Some accurate allusions are made and a good degree of textual knowledge is demonstrated, but the candidate has not capitalised on central points and there is no use of critical scholarship.

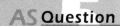

The Holy Spirit

(a) Examine the role of the Holy Spirit in the Fourth Gospel. (14 marks)

(b) Assess the importance of the Holy Spirit in the ministry of Jesus as presented in the Fourth Gospel. (6 marks)

A-grade answer to AS question 5

(a) The Holy Spirit plays a multiplicity of functions in the Fourth Gospel, indicated by the titles that the Fourth Evangelist applies to it. It appears at the beginning of Jesus's public ministry as the *pneuma* (spirit), resting and remaining on Jesus, but the terminology changes in the latter part of the gospel when Jesus promises the disciples that the *Paraclete* will come to them after his departure.

> This is vital in a discussion of the Spirit in the Fourth Gospel, displaying an awareness of the distinctive terminology used.

As early as chapter three, Jesus tells Nicodemus that new birth in water and Spirit is the only way to eternal life. A spiritual birth is the distinguishing characteristic of a disciple in whom the Spirit will come and dwell after Jesus's glorification. John makes a distinctive link between water and Spirit, and he explains that 'rivers of living water' flowing from the heart of the believer are the Spirit poured out on them after Jesus's death (John 7:39). Water therefore is not something separate from the Spirit, but a way of describing its effects and tasks. The Evangelist is picking up on the Old Testament images for thirsting for God — Psalm 42:1 for example: 'As the deer pants for flowing streams, so longs my soul for you, O God.' He sees the Spirit as the way in which this longing for God will be satisfied, and the Samaritan woman is one example of a disciple who drinks from the living spiritual water that Jesus offers.

> These early references to the Spirit tend to get overlooked. A good candidate will refer to more than the *Paraclete* passages.

The giving of the Spirit (John 20:19–23) when Jesus appears to the Eleven is another distinctive characteristic of the Fourth Gospel's presentation. *Pneuma* is used here, although it is clearly the same *Paraclete* that Jesus promised in the farewell discourses. John uses the same word play that was utilised in the conversation with Nicodemus in chapter three; wind, breath and spirit, all *pneuma* in Greek, are virtually indistinguishable until translated into English. Jesus breathes the Spirit onto the disciples in an intimate act of giving his successor to them.

> More analysis of the etymology of the terms used sets this essay apart as a high-level response.

The *Paraclete* Spirit is to be sent by the Father and the Son, proceeding from the same divine essence and sharing the same unity of purpose and nature. It is the 'presence of Jesus when he is absent' (Raymond Brown) and so can dwell within believers just as Jesus does. The world will not understand the relationship between the Spirit and the disciples, just as they did not understand Jesus himself, but for the disciples it will intercede, comfort, guide and teach, leading them into a deeper knowledge of Jesus's words. It will separate them from the world, singling the disciples out as witnesses to Jesus, and cementing the personal relationship they have with the Father and the Son.

🅔 Scholarship is introduced effectively in this paragraph.

Ultimately, the presentation of the *Paraclete* Spirit in the Fourth Gospel addressed the problem of the delay of the *Paraclete*. At the end of the first century, Jesus's anticipated return had not yet occurred, and the Church was anxious. However: 'At a critical stage in the development of the Johannine Community it had been troubled by...the delay of the *Paraclete*...John's church had solved these problems by the doctrine of the *Paraclete* as the living presence of Jesus in the church' (J. and K. Court).

(b) The Fourth Evangelist presents the Holy Spirit as important for Jesus's own ministry as well as for the future of the Church and the ministry of the disciples. When John the Baptist sees the Spirit descend and remain on Jesus this identifies Jesus as the Son of God but, more than that, as the one in whom the Spirit is permanently tabernacled in order that he might pass it on to believers. John the Witness identified Jesus as the one who would baptise in the Holy Spirit, not just in water as he had done, and with the coming of the Spirit the messianic age has now begun.

🅔 The candidate has got straight into a clear analysis of the importance of the Spirit for Jesus's own ministry. Note, of course, that this necessitates having been thoughtful about how to distribute material over parts (a) and (b).

The Spirit therefore empowers Jesus in his ministry. His signs are witness that the Spirit is with him, although he can promise to the disciples that they will accomplish greater works than he has done once the Spirit comes to dwell within them. As Elijah passed to Elisha a double portion of his Spirit, enabling him to perform even more miracles than his predecessor, so too will the disciples know no limit to what they can accomplish through the power of the Spirit passed from Jesus to them.

🅔 The candidate demonstrates good Old Testament knowledge.

Whilst the *pneuma* spirit is possessed by Jesus, the *Paraclete* is clearly 'another' like him (John 14:16), and part of the distinctiveness of the Spirit is the characteristic way in which the *Paraclete* fulfils the functions that Jesus has performed on earth. Everything that Jesus does during his ministry, the *Paraclete* will do after him, empowering and equipping the disciples as the *pneuma* spirit did Jesus.

🅔 A good combination of textual knowledge and scholarly analysis has been effectively blended, which would lead to a solid A grade.

C-grade answer to AS question 5

(a) The Holy Spirit appears frequently in the Fourth Gospel and plays an important part in the ministry of Jesus. The Holy Spirit is part of the 'Trinity' — that is, God the Father, God the Son and God the Holy Spirit. It is known by a variety of terms, first as the *pneuma*, the spirit of God that remains with Jesus, and later Jesus calls it the 'counsellor' (*Paraclete*), when he promises the disciples that the Spirit will come when he has left them.

> This is a useful beginning, showing that the candidate is aware of the terminology. However, since the Fourth Gospel does not particularly develop a doctrine of the Trinity, it is probably not really necessary to introduce this term. Better to keep to terms specifically used in the gospel, such as *pneuma* and '*Paraclete*'.

The Holy Spirit seems to be within Jesus — it comes down to him as a dove at his baptism — and in his conversation with Nicodemus, Jesus teaches that in order to gain salvation a person must 'be born of water and the spirit' (John 3:5), showing that having the Spirit within you is an important part of following Jesus and being a disciple.

> This paragraph touches on important points, but does not develop them properly. It begins with an error that many candidates make — the baptism incident is not in the Fourth Gospel. The candidate makes a very useful reference to the Spirit and Nicodemus, but needs to include much more discussion about the meaning and importance of this.

The Holy Spirit appears most prominently in the discourse with the disciples. At the Last Supper Jesus tells the disciples that he is going to leave them soon and that the Father will send the Holy Spirit to them to enable them to carry on his work. The Spirit will be a counsellor who will help them to bring the good news to all people: 'But the Counsellor, the Holy Spirit, whom the Father will send in my name, will teach you all things' (John 14:25).

He is the Spirit of Truth and is equal to Jesus himself and he will live within the disciples and help them to see and understand the truth. The world will not understand the relationship between the Spirit and the disciples, but for the followers of Jesus the Spirit will be their comforter, teacher and guide and will separate the disciples from the world.

> This shows a reasonable knowledge of the text, but it is a simple re-telling of the narrative. There needs to be some discussion of meaning and importance.

When Jesus dies on the cross, the gospel writer notes that Jesus 'gave up his Spirit' and some scholars have suggested that this refers to the breaking of the spiritual link between the Father and the Son — a link which is restored at the Resurrection.

> An interesting point — a pity it isn't developed further. As it is, its relevance is not clear.

After the Resurrection, Jesus appears to the 11 disciples and gives them the Holy Spirit. He does this by breathing on them and saying 'Receive the Holy Spirit' (John 20:22). This is linked with the notion that the Spirit is the breath of God — just as God breathed life into Adam in the Old Testament. It highlights the very close personal relationship which Jesus had with the disciples.

> This is a good conclusion to the section, with a useful Old Testament reference.

(b) The scholar Smalley says that the Holy Spirit is important in the ministry because it gives Jesus the power to carry out his task. It is his link with the Father and therefore helps him to know what the Father's will is. It also helps him to pray and to perform the miraculous signs. The Holy Spirit is the vital support that Jesus needs — without the Holy Spirit, Jesus could not have carried out his ministry.

> This paragraph contains lots of useful information and some analysis, but it is rather too condensed. The information needs to be unpacked and analysed more carefully.

Of course, the Holy Spirit is also important because the work of Jesus had to be carried on by his disciples, and the Spirit enabled them to do so — in a sense, it helped them to be like Jesus himself and enabled the Christian Church to develop.

> A rather feeble ending which says nothing new. A little scholarly analysis, perhaps on the different functions of the Holy Spirit, would have helped.

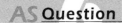
Women in the Gospels

(a) With reference to three separate incidents, examine the importance of women in the ministry of Jesus as presented in the Fourth Gospel. (14 marks)

(b) To what extent do these incidents reflect the social and religious conditions of the time? (6 marks)

A-grade answer to AS question 6

(a) Women feature prominently in the Fourth Gospel, as Raymond Brown notes: 'If other Christian communities thought of Peter as the one who made a supreme confession of Jesus as the Son of God and the one to whom the risen Lord first appeared, the Johannine community associated such memories with Martha and Mary Magdalene.' They appear in a number of guises, but always positively and as foil for the male characters, who are invariably slower to come to an understanding of who Jesus is.

> No A-grade essay is ever going to start with the phrase 'Women were considered second-class citizens in Jesus's day'. Note that this one does not.

Jesus's mother is never named in the gospel, and Joseph Grassi observes that like the Beloved Disciple she is therefore given the freedom to be a truly symbolic character who witnesses the beginning (Cana) and the end (the Cross) of Jesus's ministry. At the wedding at Cana she bears witness to his authority as she orders the servants, 'Do as he tells you', and although her understanding of Jesus's role is implicit, the Evangelist implies that she has a vital role to play in the opening scenes of his ministry. A link between the wedding and the Cross — wine, water and blood — is cemented by her appearance at the crucifixion, where she bears witness to the final act, the handing over of the Beloved Disciple to her as her son, as Jesus's true successor. She shares the Beloved Disciple's testimony and is thus part of the foundational witness upon which the Johannine community is based.

> The candidate avoids simple story-telling while ensuring that knowledge of the text is conveyed.

The Samaritan woman is one of the primary heroines of the gospel, a prototype of the ideal disciple. Although she has no obvious advantages, she is far more discerning than the learned Nicodemus, and she represents those whose faith grows from the limitations of physical and earthly understanding to real spiritual insight. She works through a limited grasp of who Jesus is to an insight that he is the Messiah that she and her fellow Samaritans have been awaiting. But even more importantly she initiates the first mass mission as she witnesses to her village. Those who respond to her testimony give no indication that they found it hard to do so because she was a woman, although interestingly, Jesus's own male disciples do wonder amongst themselves why he was talking with her, and Martin Boer suggests that this may represent the Johannine community's own internal struggles over the acceptance of women and Gentiles.

Mary Magdalene features only in the Resurrection narrative, but her role is highly significant, for she is commissioned by the risen Jesus to be 'the apostle to the apostles'. Unlike Luke and Paul, John suggests that she was the first to see Jesus, who calls her to share in the relationship he has with God ('My Father and your Father, my God and your God'), and it is the message that Jesus can no longer be limited to an earthly relationship that she takes back to the male disciples. John uses the same non-recognition motif that is found in the synoptics, as Mary first thinks Jesus to be the gardener, but this provides an opportunity for Jesus to reveal himself to her as the Good Shepherd who calls his own by name. Only when he speaks her name to her does she recognise him; he is then able to explain to her the new status that she and the others can enjoy in their relationship with him.

> All three episodes have now been covered without any descent into narrative or cliché. A strong part (a) that demonstrates excellent AO1 skills.

(b) Peter Vardy and Mary Mills observe that: 'In both pagan and Jewish society women were considered to be less intelligent than men...in the wider arena of social life, in politics, and religious affairs, women had almost no role at all.' However, it is important not to leap to the conclusion that women therefore were considered of no status whatsoever, since there are clear exceptions, as Proverbs 31 suggests — 'A woman who fears the Lord is to be praised. Give her the fruit of her hands, and let her works praise her in the gates' (31:30–31). Nevertheless, it is traditionally held that Jesus did much to raise the status of women, even if his example was not always followed in the early Church.

> The candidate has been careful to point out that we cannot categorically say that all women were at the bottom of the social pile in the first century — a line that many candidates trot out, rarely with the support of any real evidence.

In any dealings with women it is possible that Jesus held himself open to the strongest criticisms, against a cultural background in which Josephus claimed that the Law held women to be inferior in all matters. Philo of Alexandria spoke of women's characteristics as examples of weakness, and Sirach 42:14 says: 'Better is the wickedness of a man than a woman who does good.'

> This is exactly the kind of evidence that is so often lacking.

In marked contrast, Jesus welcomes contact with women, and offers them teaching that is no less theologically challenging than that which he offers to men. Furthermore, the Samaritan woman is a member of a despised race and conceivably a moral outcast from

her community; the woman caught in adultery is technically guilty of judgement under the Law. On both occasions Jesus offers them the chance to be restored to their societies and to begin a new life based on a relationship with him.

> e Good analysis backed up with concrete examples would secure an A grade for this candidate.

■ ■ ■

C-grade answer to AS question 6

(a) The incidents with the Samaritan woman, the woman caught in adultery, and the anointing at Bethany are all examples of the importance of women in the ministry of Jesus.

> e This could be interesting — not many candidates would deliberately choose the second two episodes mentioned here.

The Samaritan woman is identified by Raymond Brown as a typical Johannine disciple, as she responds positively to Jesus and then goes and witnesses about him to her village. She is initially slow to believe, however. When Jesus offers her living water she does not appreciate that he is talking about spiritual water and not water from the well where she has gone to draw at the hottest time of the day. But unlike Nicodemus, she is prepared to examine what Jesus says at a deeper level and gradually she appreciates that he is offering her something desirable: 'Give me this water that I may not thirst, nor come here to draw' (John 4:15). Jesus does not pursue the matter of water with her, however, but turns her attention to her own life and circumstances. By demonstrating his omniscience, he begins to reveal something of his identity and after he has introduced to her the concept of true worship in spirit and truth, she tentatively identifies him as the Messiah.

When the Samaritan woman goes to her village and tells them about Jesus (leaving her water jar behind, which symbolises her old life) she fulfils the most important task given to men and women in the Fourth Gospel — that of witness. The Samaritans believe in her testimony and respond positively to Jesus, and as Brown suggests she has 'reaped the apostolic harvest'.

> e This is all quite competent. The candidate has included a little scholarship and some textual allusion, but the time expended on this episode may well be at the cost of the other two.

The adulterous woman is never named and is a rather ephemeral character. She is not a disciple and we do not know what happens to her after the event, but she provides the opportunity for Jesus to teach about forgiveness and judgement. The Pharisees are looking for a chance to condemn Jesus, but he does not respond as they expect him to. He fails to condemn the woman to death, but draws attention instead to the

Pharisees' own sins, forcing the crowd to back away. When the woman is left alone with Jesus he gives her the opportunity to return to her community and begin a new life, as the Samaritan woman did.

> **ℯ** As anticipated, the candidate has provided far less detail on this episode. Perhaps it is not the best choice for this essay, as it is unlikely that as much study time has been spent on it as on the Samaritan woman.

Mary, the sister of Martha and Lazarus, performs the anointing at Bethany. She comes into her own in this account, although Martha appeared to play the dominant role at the raising of Lazarus. Her action is interpreted by Judas as merely an extravagant waste of expensive ointment, but Jesus praises her for it — 'she has kept it for the day of my burial'. This is the important feature of this account. The woman has recognised what the men in the gospel have failed to appreciate — that Jesus will die and that his death should be anticipated and prepared for in advance. It is a prophetic anointing and this is why Jesus treats her favourably.

> **ℯ** Some scholarly quotation about this episode would have been very welcome. This is an interesting and complex incident which merits discussion in greater depth.

(b) The religious and social conditions at the time were not especially favourable to women, who were accorded far less status than men and had little role to play in public life, although they were valued within the family. A woman's identity depended heavily upon the male members of her family and on motherhood, and after the birth of her first child she would be known as 'mother of...'. Graham Stanton observes: 'The status of women was remarkably inferior to that of men throughout the ancient world, including Judaism.'

> **ℯ** This candidate has not fallen into the 'second-class citizens' trap and has included a relevant scholarly quotation.

Jesus's interaction with women is therefore very significant. He goes out of his way to include them in his ministry and to ensure that others do not exclude them. He defends the adulterous woman and Mary against men, and he does not condemn the Samaritan woman for her unconventional marital history. In a society where women were far more likely than men to be accused of immorality, this is very important. Jesus seems to be setting out a mandate for the early Church which may not always have been followed, since it is possible that Paul was not as open to the role of women in the Church as Jesus appears to have been.

> **ℯ** This would benefit considerably if more connections were made between the textual material and the discussion of social circumstances. The comment about Paul is something of a red herring. This is a competent but not outstanding offering, which would gain a C grade.

Themes in the Acts of the Apostles

> **(a)** Outline the work of Peter on the Day of Pentecost. (6 marks)
>
> **(b)** Examine Peter's contribution to his meeting with Cornelius. (8 marks)
>
> **(c)** To what extent is the work of Peter important in bringing Gentiles into the early Church? (6 marks)

A-grade answer to AS question 7

(a) After the ascension of Jesus, the disciples are left to face the prospect of life without him, carrying the burden of responsibility he has left them to take the gospel to 'all nations'. A relatively small band of 120 believers are together when Peter officiates over the election of Matthias, the new twelfth apostle, but on the day of Pentecost not only do their spirits strengthen, but their numbers also grow. The Holy Spirit comes upon them, resting on them in tongues of fire and bestowing on them the gift of tongues (or *glossolalia*). Peter's singular contribution is made in response to the mocking crowd, which suggests that the disciples are drunk. Peter challenges this, not only because it is merely nine o'clock in the morning, but also because what has happened is clearly a fulfilment of scripture.

> 🄴 A good deal of information has been included in a short space here and we are given a very comprehensive picture of the circumstances of Peter's contribution.

Peter takes responsibility for addressing the crowds and gives the first public sermon of the post-Resurrection community. He cites Joel 2:28–32, claiming that the phenomenon of tongues is part of the Old Testament expectation of the 'last days' and marks the time as one to which men and women should respond with repentance. He uses the opportunity to explain the significance of Jesus's death — not a tragic accident or the deserved death of a criminal, but the 'definite plan and foreknowledge of God'. It was nevertheless the responsibility of the Jews, and Peter tells the crowd that the only appropriate response is to repent, believe, be baptised and receive the Holy Spirit. It is Jesus's crucifixion, resurrection and exaltation to the right hand of God that confirms his Messiahship and is the reason that the Holy Spirit has come to rest on Peter and the others on that day.

Three thousand new believers are added to the Church on the Day of Pentecost, indicating how powerful Peter's words have been, and his position as leader of the Church in Jerusalem is securely established.

Excellent textual knowledge is combined with an understanding of the relevance of the material.

(b) Peter's visit to Cornelius's house marks a watershed in the young Church. It is preceded by a vision in which Peter sees a sheet descending from heaven — in it 'all kinds of animals and reptiles and birds of the air'. A voice commands Peter to eat the creatures which, according to Jewish dietary laws, are unclean. As a Jewish-Christian, Peter is horrified by such a command from God, but is forced to rethink his position when he is told: 'What God has cleansed, you must not call unclean.'

Cornelius has also been prepared for this meeting. He is instructed in a vision to get ready for a visit from Peter, who has been told to go to Cornelius's house. Cornelius is overwhelmed by Peter's visit, amazed that a Jew should associate with a Gentile, who would be considered unclean. Peter tells him of his experience, and his own startling revelation that: 'Truly I perceive that God shows no partiality, but in every nation any one who fears him and does what is right is acceptable to him.' He preaches to Cornelius essentially the same message that he gave out at Pentecost, underlining the fact that the gospel of salvation is rooted in Jewish tradition and experience, even while it is open to all men.

ⓔ It is difficult to do anything except expound the narrative here, but this has been done fluently and with some explanation of its significance at the end of the paragraph.

Even while he is still speaking, the Holy Spirit comes down on all who are listening, bringing with it the gift of tongues. Peter is further convinced that the gospel message is therefore for all people, and that if the Holy Spirit is free to baptise them then they cannot be refused water baptism.

(c) This episode demonstrates just how important Peter's role is in bringing Gentiles into the Church. Although Paul is traditionally considered the apostle to the Gentiles, Peter effectively ministers over the first Gentile mission in the conversion of Cornelius and paves the way for the great Gentile mission associated with Paul. Marshall states that 'Acts reflects the tremendous tensions which existed in the early church over the basis of the Gentile mission', and Peter's role in bringing Gentiles into the Church is especially significant, since he was so firmly established as the Jewish-Christian leader in Jerusalem. His willingness to accept what God has declared clean is vital for the future spread of the Church.

ⓔ It is important to avoid repeating material from the other sections here, and the candidate has managed to do this by moving on to the Council of Jerusalem.

Interestingly, although Paul speaks in Galatians of having to take Peter to task for refusing to eat with Gentiles (Marshall observes that Peter found his new stance hard to maintain consistently), Peter stands up before the Council at Jerusalem to claim that he himself has declared that God makes no distinction between Jews and Gentiles for the purposes of salvation. He is convinced that the Council must not place an unbearable 'yoke upon the neck of the disciples' in requiring them to submit to circumcision, but that all men are saved 'through the grace of the Lord Jesus'. It is Paul's and Barnabas's contributions that support Peter's rather than the other way around, but the cumulative force of their testimony ensures that Gentiles will be permitted into the Church without the requirement of circumcision.

This is good, well-rounded coverage of the material would yield a solid A grade.

■ ■ ■

C-grade answer to AS question 7

(a) On the day of Pentecost, Peter is with the other disciples in Jerusalem. In the house where they are staying a wind rushes through and tongues of fire appear to settle on each of them and they are filled with the Holy Spirit and begin to speak in tongues of strange languages. They run out into the street where the people watching are amazed and some even think that they are drunk: 'All of them were filled with the Holy Spirit' (Acts 2:4).

A good start, with a clear outline of the opening events.

Peter then speaks to the crowd at great length. He tells them that the people are not drunk and that what is happening was prophesied in the Old Testament: 'God says, I will pour out my Spirit on all people' (Acts 2:17).

He then goes on to tell them about the ministry of Jesus and how God has raised him from the dead. He calls on the people to repent and ask God for forgiveness, and many people are converted.

This is a fair account, although rather cramped. A little more detail would help.

(b) Peter visits Cornelius after receiving a vision from God. Until this time, the members of the early Church have followed Jewish dietary laws. Peter's vision is of a large sheet coming down from above containing all kinds of animals and a voice telling him to 'Kill and eat' (Acts 13:13). When he awakes, he meets some men who have come from Cornelius, a Roman centurion, with an invitation to Peter to come to his house. Peter goes, even though it is against the Jewish law to associate with a Gentile. Cornelius is a god-fearing man, who has received a vision from God that he should talk with Peter. As he speaks to Cornelius, Peter realises that God is telling him that the Church should be open to all people and not just the Jews. He says that 'God does not show favouritism' (Acts 10:34). As he speaks, the Holy Spirit comes down on them all. They become the first Gentile believers.

This is a clear, factual paragraph with accurate reference to the text and useful quotations, although it could do with more detail. A little more background information would be helpful.

(c) The work of Peter is vital in bringing Gentiles into the early Church. Originally, the leaders of the Church thought that the followers of Jesus could only be Jews, since Jesus was himself a Jew and they were also Jews. This meant that believers had to obey Jewish laws, particularly those concerned with food and circumcision. The problem was that this left out the rest of the world — the Gentiles. Peter's work is vital, as he introduces the first Gentile believer, Cornelius, and following his vision with the sheet and animals, begins to convince the leaders of the Church that Jewish dietary laws no longer apply. This is important — if Jewish laws do not apply, then members of the Church need not be Jews, and Gentiles can be admitted. At the Council of Jerusalem, where the whole issue is discussed, Peter speaks up in favour of admitting Gentiles into the Church: 'God, who knows the heart, showed he accepted them by giving the Holy Spirit to them, just as he did to us' (Acts 15:8).

The Council agrees and this leads the way for Gentiles to be admitted. Peter's role is therefore crucial in beginning the spread of the early Church around the world.

🄴 There is some attempt at assessing the importance of Peter here, but analytical scholarship is lacking. The candidate relies rather heavily on textual narrative and is inclined to be repetitious.

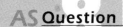

The Resurrection Narratives

> **(a)** Explain two religious differences between the Resurrection Narratives as presented in the gospels of Mark and John. (14 marks)
>
> **(b)** 'Mark's gospel is only concerned with history. John's gospel is more concerned with theology.' To what extent is this a valid judgement? (6 marks)

A-grade answer to AS question 8

(a) Mark's short account of the resurrection (assuming that 16:9–20 is a later addition, based on other accounts) leaves far more to the imagination than it discloses. It is told entirely from the point of view of the women who go to the tomb to anoint Jesus, discussing who will move the stone, only to find, to their surprise, that it has already been moved. They are greeted by an otherwise unidentified man in white (an angel perhaps) who tells them abruptly that they are looking in the wrong place for Jesus. He appears almost to rebuke them for visiting the tomb, since Jesus told them that he would be raised and would see them in Galilee. However, despite his commission to them to pass on this astounding news to Peter and the other disciples, they leave the tomb silently, saying nothing, 'for they were afraid'.

> **e** The candidate presents the narrative details simply and accurately. This is a stylish answer.

This abrupt ending is a striking and distinctive feature of the gospel, since it implies that the resurrection message was not made known. Of course, it was, and the women's silence as they left the tomb did not silence it for ever. Why then end the gospel on such a terse note? Morna Hooker suggests that the ambiguity serves to invite readers to make their own journey to Galilee to encounter the risen Christ. The ending is left open not because the message is ultimately unspoken but so that each reader can appropriate it for themselves.

> **e** Good analysis of the narrative, which shows that the candidate is aware of its significance.

Hence there are no resurrection appearances in the traditional ending of the gospel. We are given no information as to how and when Jesus did meet with Peter and the others, which was evidently a matter of some concern for early Church scribes. The additional endings represent a pastiche of appearances taken from other gospel accounts which elaborate rather poetically on the simple Marcan account of 16:1–8.

e Wisely, the candidate has chosen not to get drawn into lengthy discussion of the alternative endings.

In contrast, the Fourth Gospel account spans two chapters and includes a range of appearances, although chapter 21 is likely to be an epilogue to the gospel added some time later. Here the only woman to feature is Mary Magdalene, and while the others have been written out of the narrative, Peter and the Beloved Disciple take their place. The Beloved Disciple is singled out as the first to grasp the significance of the folded grave clothes and the empty tomb, while Peter's response appears less certain. Unlike the Marcan women, Mary Magdalene meets the risen Jesus and is obedient to her important commission to 'go to my brothers and say to them, I am ascending to my Father and your Father...'. As is characteristic in accounts written by the Fourth Evangelist, it is a woman who receives and responds to a deeply significant encounter with Jesus.

e The candidate has made a good job of comparing two religious features: the discovery of the empty tomb and the subsequent appearances — or lack of them.

Unlike Mark too, there are three important resurrection appearances that serve to tidy up the loose ends of the gospel. Thomas's unbelief offers Jesus the opportunity to give a special blessing 'to those who have not seen and yet believe', and Thomas's confession of Jesus as 'My Lord and My God' is the highest Christological confession of the gospel. On the shore of Tiberias Jesus calls Peter to the service of a pastor, and Peter's three-fold confession of love for Jesus cancels out his earlier denials. Thus the Resurrection Narrative of John is dense with material that the simple Marcan account ignores. Although, after the triumph of the cross, John barely needs a Resurrection Narrative, Smalley writes of it: 'This is the heart of the matter...the new age of fulfilment is here, and Judaism has been replaced by Christianity'.

(b) This statement reflects an outdated view of the gospels, most particularly that Mark's is nothing more than a short biography of Jesus that displays no interest in theology. As the first of the gospels to be written, and the framework upon which Matthew and Luke drew, it was long held that Mark was the Cinderella gospel, which could offer nothing in the way of deeper theological insights. However, a deep interest in Christology can be traced through the gospel, starting from the prologue (Mark 1:1–13), which introduces Jesus as the Son of God and culminates in the centurion's confession at the foot of the cross in 15:39 — 'Truly this man was the Son of God'. J. D. Kingsbury comments that while there may be traces of a messianic secret running throughout the gospel, there is certainly a revelation of it also.

e This is the tricky part of the question, which could trouble a weaker candidate. Here, however, textual knowledge and scholarship are firmly juxtaposed.

Throughout the gospel, the Evangelist constantly presents Jesus as the one who is on earth to display God's power and authority — over sin, sickness, demons, the sea, even death itself. The crowds are amazed, asking 'Who is this?' The reader, however, is in no doubt as to who Jesus is, since all the information required to answer that question has been given in the first 13 verses. Mark has a theological agenda and although his gospel may be brief, it is not a simple biography.

The Fourth Gospel was described by Clement of Alexandria as a 'spiritual gospel', and as a supplement to the Synoptic gospels it may appear that it was intended to make theological points at the expense of historical accuracy. The cleaning of the temple and the death of Jesus are timed differently to the Synoptics, emphasising important theological points about the ministry of Jesus and its relationship to Judaism. The gospel's high Christology, the reduced number of miracles, and the development of discourses all suggest that the gospel was written for specific theological purposes.

> e This is all vital material, which could have been developed further, but the candidate has provided just the right amount of detail.

However, we are not in a position to assume that the Fourth Gospel is not interested in history at all. Jesus's ministry is still set against a background of recognisable historical characters and geographical settings, and betrays the political and religious climate of its time. Furthermore, the Evangelists would be aware that without a valid historical framework to their writings the theological significance would inevitably be undermined. Both Evangelists are historians and theologians, although their theological perspective necessarily influences their view of history, as is the case for all the biblical writers.

> e A thoughtful conclusion brings another A-grade essay to a neat ending.

■ ■ ■

C-grade answer to AS question 8

(a) The Resurrection Narratives in the Fourth Gospel are much longer than those in Mark's gospel and contain far more detail. Firstly, in Mark, the women go to the tomb to anoint Jesus's body after burial, but when they get there they discover that the tomb is empty. They encounter a young man in white (is he the man who ran away from the Garden of Gethsemane?) who tells them not to look for Jesus there because, as he told them he would, he has risen and gone before them into Galilee. The women are told to go and tell 'Peter and the disciples' that Jesus has risen. However, they do not.

> e What's going on here? The essay does not make clear yet what the two religious differences are, and there is a danger that the candidate will just recount all that he or she can remember about the Resurrection Narratives.

In the Fourth Gospel, only Mary Magdalene is described as being at the tomb, although the author may simply have excluded mention of the other women who were not important to him. As soon as she finds the tomb empty she tells Peter and the Beloved Disciple, who go to investigate. They see the folded grave clothes, and the Beloved

Disciple, who is always the first to recognise the significance of events, understands that this means Jesus has been raised from the dead. They go to tell the others, and Mary is left alone.

e There is some good factual knowledge here, but that is all it is.

Jesus appears to Mary but she at first thinks he is the gardener. This lack of recognition is a typical feature of Resurrection Narratives, and it may be explained in various ways. Firstly, Mary was not expecting to see Jesus and so is unprepared to recognise him, but secondly, it is important that those who see the risen Jesus are ready to understand new teachings, and if they are excited by recognising him straight away, this may be missed. Jesus leads Mary gradually into recognising him by calling her name, just as the Good Shepherd calls his sheep, and she can then recognise him as *Rabboni* — teacher.

e The candidate has made some attempt at analysis, but it is still unclear what the two religious differences between the gospels are.

The key difference between the account in Mark and the account in the Fourth Gospel therefore is that in Mark there is no real statement of understanding that Jesus has risen, and the women are too afraid to say anything, whereas in the Fourth Gospel the Beloved Disciple immediately understands and Mary is given a commission by Jesus to which she immediately responds.

e Finally two religious differences have been identified, but because this answer is so heavily narrative-based, they have been very hard to unpack.

Another key difference is that there are no resurrection appearances at all in Mark. In the Fourth Gospel, after Jesus has appeared to Mary, he also appears to the inner circle of disciples (twice, since Thomas was not present at the first appearance) and breathes on them the Holy Spirit. He then appears yet again, at the miraculous catch of fish on the Sea of Tiberius and when he commissions Peter to feed his sheep. This appearance also serves as an opportunity to explain why the Beloved Disciple had to die.

However, in Mark's account the only appearances are those which are in the added endings, and they are presumably there because later editors of the gospel felt it strange that there were none. The ending of Mark at 16:8 could be thought unsatisfactory as it leaves everything hanging in the air, whereas in John there are effectively two endings (at the end of chapters 20 and 21) and the chapters are used to clarify a number of important points.

e In these closing stages there is some attempt at analysis, but it is rather late in the day and, overall, the candidate has made heavy weather of the answer.

(b) Mark's gospel is the earliest gospel and for this reason it could easily be thought not to be interested in theology. Although it was originally thought that Matthew might have written first, by the early twentieth century scholars generally agreed that Mark had written first, and that Luke and Matthew had used his gospel along with their own sources in producing theirs. Almost all of Mark is included in Matthew and Luke, and their most profound theology and characteristic interests and themes are from the material derived from their own sources — L and M — and not from the Marcan material.

Matthew and Luke also made use of another source not available to Mark — Q, or *Quelle*, meaning 'source'. This otherwise unknown document contains sayings of Jesus and material about John the Baptist and some parables not found in Mark.

> This could be relevant, but we need to see how it will be related to the issue raised in the question.

All this has led scholars to speculate about the nature and purpose of Mark and to suggest that the Evangelist had no interest in theological matters but was only concerned to give the simplest narrative account of Jesus's ministry. However, more recently, scholars have been aware that there are other deeper levels to Mark's account, and that it places great importance on the Christology of Jesus as Son of God. The Passion Narratives are given great significance, leading to the famous description of Mark as a Passion Narrative with an extended introduction. Mark's gospel also seems to have originated the messianic secret — the failure of people, disciples included, to recognise who Jesus is.

> This is fine, but some specific textual examples and a scholarly quotation would have given it real substance.

If, therefore, Mark has more theology than may have been supposed, is it true that John is not concerned with history? Certainly, John may well be more concerned to draw out the theological significance of certain episodes. The cleansing of the temple is at the beginning of the gospel, which may be to emphasise that it shows how Jesus will transform Judaism, and there are three Passovers, which are conveniently placed as the background for certain episodes that have a Passover theme. John spends more time dealing with discourses than activities of Jesus. However, if John was written before the Synoptics, there is no reason to suggest that these may not be historically accurate. If he was close to the events as an eyewitness, this would also be grounds for supposing that his gospel includes more history than has been assumed. So there is some reason for saying that John is more interested in theology and Mark in history but, in reality, they are probably interested in both.

> Ultimately, the candidate has answered the question, but the approach has been very uneconomical and it has taken a lot of hard work to reach a high C grade.

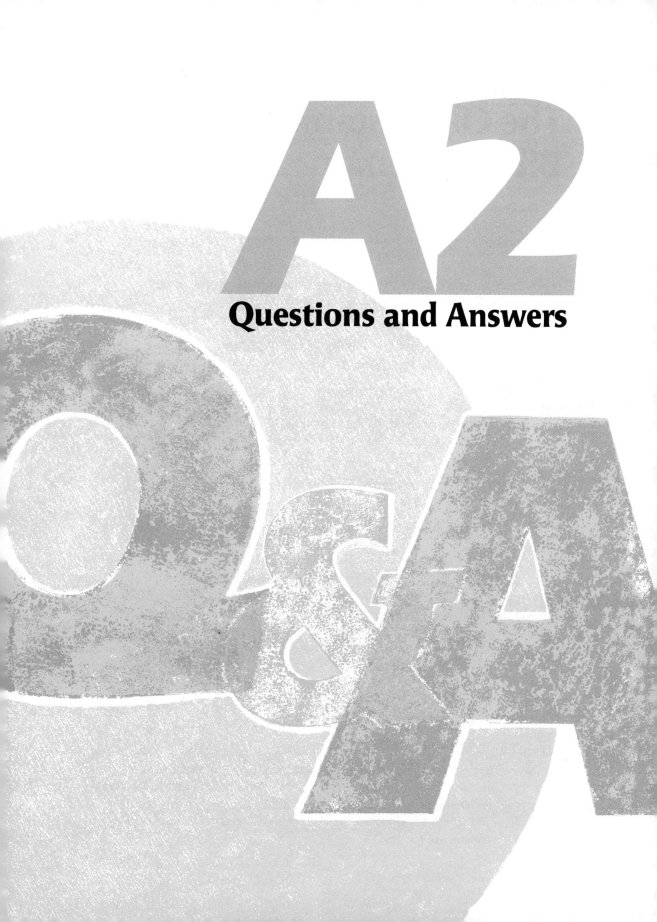

A2
Questions and Answers

The Old Testament/Jewish Bible: Solomon

> **(a)** Discuss and analyse the reasons why Solomon has been considered a successful king. (10 marks)
>
> **(b)** Examine and analyse the arguments that suggest that Solomon is ultimately a failure. (10 marks)

A-grade answer to A2 question 1

(a) Solomon's reign begins with enormous hope, and building on the tremendous popularity of his father before him, Solomon's position is strong. David has defeated all Israel's enemy nations, and Solomon simply has to sit back and enjoy the tribute they bring in. He fights no battles and faces no economic or political threats to his reign.

> *e* This question concerns a popular topic and deserves to be answered well. Narrative detail must be conveyed with an understanding of the implications of what happens in Solomon's reign.

Solomon is the first king to ascend the throne by lineage. He is therefore not a charismatic leader but a king 'born to the purple', whose background is the luxury of the court, not the rustic battlefield. However, Solomon capitalises on the military strength of Israel built up by David and establishes vital trading links with other nations, most particularly with King Hiram of Tyre and Sidon and the Queen of Sheba. As a result, during Solomon's reign Israel gains in political, cultural and commercial prestige, and Solomon establishes an enormous court and an equally impressive domestic and political system to support it. The court's wealth is of direct benefit to the people of the nation, who reap the rewards of Solomon's commercial strategies and the savings made by not having to go out to battle: 'Judah and Israel were as many as the sand by the sea; they ate and drank and were happy' (1 Kings 4:20).

> *e* An understanding of the significance of these textual details comes across in the way the candidate relates them.

Solomon is famed too for his wisdom, although there are doubtless elements of legend in this. Numerous songs and proverbs are attributed to him, and he is recognised by 'all Israel' for his wise judgements. Solomon's wealth, culture and prestige lead even the Queen of Sheba into despondency, because her own land and court cannot begin to equal the grandeur of his.

The building of the temple is attributed to Solomon, and much of the account of his reign is devoted to a description of its construction. Solomon exploits his relationship with Hiram of Tyre for luxury wood and labourers for the task, and the project appears to be outstripped in its grandeur only by Solomon's own palace. The temple appears to serve to unify Israel further and its dedication is a splendid affair, blessed by God himself, who fills the temple with his glory.

> ⓔ The candidate has had the sense to anticipate the second half of the question, holding back some information until reaching it, but preparing the ground for it very well.

(b) Outwardly, therefore, Solomon's reign appears to be a resounding success, establishing Israel as the powerful nation that was envisaged when the elders approached Samuel for a king. However, John Drane observes that 'judged by the standards of world powers, Solomon was outstandingly successful, the greatest of all Israel's rulers. But judged by the moral and spiritual standards of the covenant, he was a miserable failure'. The Deuteronomistic editors are careful in their telling of the story. Solomon's reign is narrated without critical comment until 1 Kings 11, when we learn that Solomon not only marries several hundred women from the surrounding pagan nations, but builds altars for the gods, and even joins his wives in their worship. Solomon enters into marriage alliances in order to cement commercial relationships with other nations, but the marriages inevitably undermine his commitment to Yahweh. This is sufficient to lead to the division of the kingdom at Solomon's death, although out of loyalty to David, Yahweh preserves the united kingdom for the rest of Solomon's reign.

> ⓔ The bulk of scholarship has been saved up for this part of the answer too, which is perfectly legitimate at this level.

As we read the text we are shown the other side of Solomon's apparently successful reign. As a dynastic king he has no way of identifying with the people he rules, using them as a means to support his court rather than seeking to ensure their loyalty to him. Furthermore, he demonstrates no respect for the old tribal divisions, using them as convenient tax-district demarcations. The loyalty of a united Israel to king and Jerusalem was a fragile thing, and Sheba's revolt during the reign of David (2 Samuel 20) is 'a splendid illustration of the fragile nature of that union and a forerunner of its eventual dissolution' (John Bright).

> ⓔ A good understanding of the implications of events prior to Solomon's reign is demonstrated here.

Inevitably, the people resent Solomon's casual disregard of the old tribal loyalties and of the freedom they had under the old confederacy. Solomon's reign is an uncannily accurate fulfilment of Samuel's warnings in 1 Samuel 8, when the elders of Israel asked for a king. It is the inevitable outcome of a request that went directly against the theocratic nature of Israel's origins and that grew out of Israel's identification with other nations, first by having a king, and subsequently by assuming the characteristics that go with monarchy. The northern elders prefer that a king should be chosen by God, just as the judges were chosen, rather than gain the throne through inheritance and political wrangling. Ultimately, at Solomon's death, the northern tribes seize the opportunity to break away from the control exercised by the increasingly powerful Davidic dynasty in Jerusalem.

> The essay concludes with a strong sense that the candidate has seen Solomon and his reign in the context of the whole monarchy. It would earn a well deserved A grade.

■ ■ ■

C-grade answer to A2 question 1

(a) Solomon's reign is a mixed blessing for Israel, but there are many reasons why he has been considered a good king. Firstly, Solomon inherits a peaceful land from David and this means that he does not have to spend time and resources going to war. He stays in Jerusalem, building up commercial and diplomatic links with other nations and establishing a reputation for Israel that makes it a nation to be respected in the Ancient Near East.

Everything is established early on in Solomon's reign to give him every possible advantage. The enemies who challenged his succession are dealt with, and when God offers to give him anything he wants, he chooses wisdom. This humble request — rather than riches and prosperity — wins him favour with God, who grants him both wisdom and wealth. Everything bodes well for the future.

> This is a solid narrative, but with no flair or analysis. This candidate is dealing with essentially the same material as the previous candidate, but the difference in the quality of treatment is clear.

Solomon establishes a court that is the equal of the courts of the great oriental kings, with many advisors and aides, and the rich agriculture of a very fertile land to call upon. His court is amply provided for and he must appear enormously impressive to surrounding nations. His trading links with Hiram of Tyre and the diplomatic visit from the Queen of Sheba indicate that he is considered to be a king of some significance in the ancient world.

Solomon builds the temple, which is undoubtedly a very important gesture. God had assured David that although he would not build the temple himself, his son would, and it is a temple of such magnificence that it clearly demonstrates that the monarchy has grown immensely in power and status since the reign of Saul.

Finally, the peace and prosperity enjoyed during Solomon's reign are not just for the court but for the people as well, and we are told that every man sits under his own fig tree — Israel has become a population of landowners.

(b) However, all is not as rosy as this picture suggests and scholars are quick to point out that Solomon has become so isolated from the common people that he no longer identifies with their needs and their circumstances. Most of all, the old tribal boundaries which were once the basis of Israel's identity are overridden as Solomon turns them into tax districts with responsibility for providing for the court. Every month a district has to supply the court with huge amounts of produce: 60 cors of flour, 10 oxen, 20 cattle, and so on.

Furthermore, Solomon introduces slave labour, which is likely to include Israelites as well as conquered peoples, the primary purpose of which is to build not only the temple but Solomon's own house. He seems to spend longer on building his own house than on building the temple, and inevitably this is offensive to the people of the land. Solomon is becoming a king like those Samuel warned against in 1 Samuel 8. He is an oriental despot who takes advantage of his nation's wealth and prosperity in order to build up his own reputation.

Under the conditions of the covenant, Israel is forbidden to worship any pagan gods, but, in the interests of building an international reputation, Solomon marries many foreign women and builds altars at which they worship their gods. Inevitably, he ends up worshipping them too and this is his downfall. In 1 Kings 11 we are told that Solomon's apostasy will destroy the unity of the kingdom. After his death, the kingdom will be divided and the north will fall into non-Davidic hands. Sure enough, when his son refuses to agree to lighten the heavy load that Solomon has placed upon the people of Israel, the north accedes and only two tribes are left for David's descendants. All in all, therefore, Solomon's reign has a lot of outward glamour and success, but ultimately it is a failure for Israel and for the Davidic monarchy.

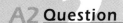

The prophetic literature: the Book of Hosea

> **(a)** Examine the message of Hosea on God's judgement of Israel. (10 marks)
>
> **(b)** Explain and analyse the importance of Hosea's teaching on God's love and reconciliation. (10 marks)

A-grade answer to A2 question 2

(a) 'Their heart is false; now they must bear their guilt. The Lord will break down their altars and destroy their pillars' (Hosea 10:2). Hosea wrote at a time when the political situation of the Northern Kingdom was in turmoil and the king, Manahem, was forced to pay an oppressive levy to the Assyrians. Hosea sees the situation as being the inevitable outcome of years of lack of fidelity to Yahweh and of worshipping pagan gods. The covenant relationship has broken down and Israel now has to pay the price.

> **e** Some simple background to Hosea's circumstances places the essay accurately in context.

Hosea sees the blame for Israel's fate lying in a number of places: the corrupt priesthood, the kings and the people. He condemns the priests and kings, who should have set an example as leaders, for allowing their people to be led astray by false idols and dependency upon other nations rather than upon God. 'Hear this, O priests! Give heed, O house of Israel! Hearken, O house of the king! For the judgement pertains to you...' (Hosea 5:1). The judgement will, however, fall on the whole nation and not just on the leaders and, if it is ultimately to be beneficial, it is vital that Israel learns from it.

> **e** Two accurate references so far suggest that the candidate is really familiar with the text.

The judgement is illustrated in the first chapter of the book in symbolic terms. Hosea's marriage to a Canaanite cultic prostitute parallels God's relationship with Israel, and their children are all given symbolic names which reflect the coming judgement: Jezreel ('God pursues in search of vengeance') reflecting Jehu's massacre in the valley of Jezreel; Lo-Ruhamah ('not pitied') indicative of God's failing patience with his apostate people; and Lo-Ammi ('not my people') — an ironic reversal of the covenant promise. The symbolism of husband and wife, father and children, underscores the fact that in judging Israel God is bringing to an end — albeit temporarily — a relationship that was personal and deeply significant.

e It may be tempting to start with Hosea's marriage, but bringing it into the essay a little later is a good way of avoiding the obvious.

Hosea chooses Exodus imagery to describe the imminent judgement. As when they came out of Egypt, the Israelites are to be faced with a desert and a time of wandering. This will be in sharp contrast to the fertile lands they have occupied but the fertility of which they ironically attributed to Baal and not to Yahweh: 'I will lay waste her vines and her fig trees, of which she said, "These are my hire, which my lovers have given me"...And I will punish her for the feast days of the Baals when she burned herself with her ring and jewelry and went after her lovers, and forgot me, says the Lord' (Hosea 2:13). The Exodus time was one in which Israel's relationship with God was established, and it will be so again, but first the Israelites must experience the judgement of Yahweh at the hands of enemy nations: 'They shall return to the land of Egypt, and Assyria shall be their king' (Hosea 11:5). Having depended upon other nations rather than on Yahweh, the Israelites must now bear the consequences: other nations will rule over them and separate them from their land. The kings whom they were so anxious to serve ('They made kings, but not through me', Hosea 8:4) have utterly failed them and they must once again recognise their complete dependence upon God if they are to survive the Exile and return to their land.

e The vital Exodus theme is expounded here.

(b) Von Rad writes of Hosea's message on salvation: 'Can we be sure that the men to whom he announced the judgement and those to whom he spoke of the coming salvation are the same in both cases? It is enough to say that...Hosea quite undoubtedly also spoke of a coming salvation.'

e Beginning with a scholarly quotation is a useful device and provides some structure to an answer.

Underlying the message of judgement is a message of God's love and reconciliation. The purpose of judgement is that Israel might learn that her covenant relationship with God is the basis on which she must go forward again, and that only by living in complete dependency on Yahweh can she be healed and restored. The Israelites will relive the Exodus experience, but this time not as a judgement but as the honeymoon period that they enjoyed with God when they came out of Egypt and the covenant was formed.

Hosea uses images of marriage again, but this time they are positive: 'I will betroth you in righteousness and justice, in love and compassion. I will betroth you in faithfulness, and you will acknowledge the Lord' (Hosea 2:19–20). God's aim is that Israel will realise that the blessings it believed were due to Baal are due to his love and faithfulness, his sovereignty and control: 'Then she shall say, "I will go and return to my first husband, for it was better with me than now". And she did not know that it was I who gave her the grain, the wine, and the oil...' (Hosea 2:7–8). Hosea's own experience with Gomer — her unfaithfulness leads to a period of separation, after which he is reconciled to her — mirrors that of God and Israel, and it is generally considered to be no coincidence that God called the prophet to undergo an experience which was a living parable. Doubtless it was a real marriage, for as Mays observes, it would be ridiculous to speak of Hosea undergoing the pain of Gomer's unfaithfulness if all the time he was 'living happily in bosom of his family'.

e More good use of both textual material and scholarly analysis.

Throughout the book, the message of reconciliation underlies the message of judgement. God's love for Israel motivates his judgement, but he does not find it easy to judge the people whom he loves: 'How can I give up on you Ephraim! How can I hand you over, O Israel...My heart recoils within me, my compassion grows warm and tender' (Hosea 11:8). It is no easy thing for God to punish Israel, but he does so as a parent punishes his child — as an act of loving discipline: 'When Israel was a child, I loved him, and out of Egypt I called my son' (Hosea 11:1). After discipline, Israel will repent and return to God. Anderson writes: 'The wilderness was to be the scene of the renewal of the covenant and there the long history of the broken covenant would be ended...Israel would answer Yahweh's overture of love.'

e Even more impressive knowledge of text and scholarship is being displayed here.

Hosea devotes the whole of chapter 14 (which may be a later addition) to a message of hope couched in the language of fertility and abundance. God's loving judgement will be vindicated by Israel's return to faithful covenant commitment, and never again will Israel be seduced by the Baals or by dependence upon other nations.

e This is an exceptionally good response to a question that could easily turn into an unconnected list of points. It is well structured and thoughtfully concluded.

■ ■ ■

C-grade answer to A2 question 2

(a) Hosea lived around 750 BCE. At that time the situation was very troubled. The Assyrian army was conquering much of the region and in the northern kingdom of Israel King Manahem was forced to pay very heavy tribute to the Assyrians. In fact, the people of Israel had only themselves to blame because they had not trusted in God and instead had been worshipping idols. A scholar noted that the people only worshipped God in order to 'get something out of religion', such as prosperity and safety.

e This is a good, if slightly lengthy, introduction which sets the scene quite well. However, it would greatly help if the candidate could name the scholar mentioned — Bernhard Anderson.

Hosea's message to the people in this situation is that God will judge them and that, afterwards, there will be a time of hope. He says that the people no longer know God and that the old covenant relationship is over. He uses his own personal life to highlight his message; he married an adulteress called Gomer and he named their three children

Jezreel, after a massacre, Lo-Ruhamah, meaning 'not pitied', which showed how God's patience had run out with Israel, and Lo-Ammi, which means 'not my people' and shows how God had rejected the people of Israel.

e This is useful information, but more discussion of the symbolism would help. What massacre? Was Gomer an adulteress before or during her marriage? Is she better understood as a Canaanite cultic prostitute?

Hosea later rejected Gomer because of her unfaithfulness, showing how God will reject Israel. Hosea blames the priests for much of the corruption in Israel. He says that God will judge the people because they have forgotten him — they have no faith, and spend their time lying, murdering, stealing and committing adultery. They do not acknowledge the sovereignty of God or their obligations under the covenant. They are sinners and so they will face God's punishment for their wickedness: 'My God will reject them because they have not obeyed him' (Hosea 9:17).

e This is a solid enough answer, although it lacks the depth of detail and discussion needed for the highest grades. For example, more could be said about how God will punish the people through the Assyrians. Closer reference to the text is also needed.

(b) Hosea's message is not all about judgement. God's love for his people is so great that he could never really desert them. God is disappointed by their sinfulness and lack of faith, and the purpose of his judgement is to lead the people to repent and come back to him. God will not destroy his people, and in their suffering, he will heal them and restore their faith. The relationship between God and his people will no longer be like a husband and wife, but more like a parent and child. God's punishment of the people will be like a parent punishing their child, as an act of love and discipline: 'When Israel was a child, I loved him' (Hosea 11:1).

Hosea teaches that God's love for his people is so great that the people will return to him and there will be a new covenant, based on that love. Anderson states that the covenant would be made when 'Israel would answer Yahweh's overture of love'.

e This information is correct, but it is rather general. The candidate makes a good point concerning the parent/child relationship, but needs to analyse the importance of the teaching much more, for example by discussing the nature of the changing relationship and the new covenant.

In fact, Hosea's message came true. King Hoshea of Israel rebelled against the Assyrians and refused to pay the tribute. A couple of years later the Assyrians conquered Israel and thousands of Israelites were taken away into slavery.

e This ending rounds off a creditable middle-range essay, but the candidate's response to (b) is far too brief.

The New Testament: the purpose of the Gospels

'Luke wants all people to understand the universal nature of God's love.'
Discuss and analyse this view of the purpose of Luke's gospel. (20 marks)

A-grade answer to A2 question 3

'A particular feature of Luke's narrative which can shed light on the nature of the community and society for whom he writes is the concern for the weak and downtrodden, the sinners, and the despised' (J. and K. Court).

It is possible that Luke was writing for a privileged audience: rich and influential Roman converts or those who had expressed an interest in knowing more about the gospel, Jesus and the impact that Christianity was likely to have on a largely Gentile society. However, even if this is the case, Luke does not sanitise his message to make it acceptable to the wealthy and well connected. On the contrary, he makes clear from the very beginning that the gospel is a universal message that requires a universal response. Gentiles, women, social outcasts, the sick and the poor are all given centre stage in Luke's gospel, which is written with a clear emphasis on the message that 'all flesh shall see the salvation of God' (Luke 3:6).

e Essays on this topic can quickly degenerate into waffle unless given a clear structure and direction. This candidate has sufficient textual knowledge and understanding of the gospel to ensure that the essay has focus from the start.

Luke begins the gospel with a dedication to an otherwise unknown figure — Theophilus. Much debate has centred on who this character may be: a Roman patron, a Gentile convert, an official to whom Luke is providing Paul's defence, or even simply a 'lover of God'. If we suppose him to be a Roman official or patron, then the purpose of the gospel suggested by this question is likely to be accurate. Luke was aware that Judaism had essentially rejected the gospel and as a companion of Paul he knew that the message had gone out to the Gentiles, where it had flourished. The gospel is written in the light of this, and anticipates the successful Gentile mission that characterises Luke's second volume, Acts. Hence, even in the temple when Jesus is presented as a baby, Simeon prophesies that he will be a 'light to the Gentiles' and the salvation that God has 'prepared in the presence of all peoples'.

e A large amount of well-learned information is dealt with quickly and efficiently here so that the essay does not lose direction.

Non-Jewish characters are presented positively, not least the centurion whose servant is ill. The Jewish elders support his appeal to Jesus: 'He is worthy to have you do this for him, for he loves our nations and built us our synagogue' (Luke 7:4). Pilate himself is presented sympathetically, declaring three times that Jesus is innocent, and delivering Jesus to be crucified only when the Jews have forced his hand. At the foot of the cross the centurion on guard declares: 'Surely this man is innocent', while the Jewish people leave the scene, beating their breasts in remorse for their part in the drama.

e In response to a question of this kind there is no substitute for thorough textual knowledge, relevantly applied.

Throughout the gospel, characters who would usually be on the fringes of society feature prominently in parables or in incidents: Zacchaeus, the tax collector up the tree, who would have been hated by his fellow Jews for collaborating with Roman power, is declared a 'son of Abraham'; the only healed leper to return to thank Jesus is a Samaritan; the woman who lost a coin and the shepherd who lost a sheep are not the most obvious heroes for a Jewish audience. All this serves to underline Luke's interest in demonstrating the universal nature of God's love. No one is excluded, and all are included.

This inclusiveness extends to the Jews. Salvation has not been lost to them; it is universally offered to all. In the parable of the lost son, the older son who so resents the joy expressed at his brother's return is not excluded from his father's love: 'Son, you are always with me, and all that is mine is yours' (Luke 15:31). However, he finds it difficult to accept that his father's love can embrace him and his renegade brother. Luke's message is that God's love reaches out to all men and women, whatever their lineage or lifestyle but, inevitably, those who cannot understand this will find themselves excluded, not because God intended them to be so, but because their attitude makes it impossible for them to receive the gospel. The parable of the great banquet (Luke 14:15–24) makes this clear: those who refuse the invitation to the kingdom must not be surprised to find that others take their places.

e This candidate displays knowledge without losing sight of the overall question or dwelling too long on a single episode.

Luke has established these themes at the beginning of the gospel. Mary's Magnificat (Luke 1:46–55) speaks of how God will lift up the lowly, fill the hungry and show mercy to all generations. Morna Hooker observes how this provides a reliable introduction to the gospel as a whole: 'We will not be surprised, later in the Gospel, to find Jesus declaring that he has come to seek out and save the lost; nor will we be surprised to learn that the humble and the outcast find a place in the Kingdom of God, while the arrogant and mighty are excluded.'

The apostles are prepared for a ministry that will fulfil God's universal plan of salvation history. As Jesus commissions them before his ascension, they are instructed that 'repentance and forgiveness of sins should be preached in his name to all nations, beginning from Jerusalem'. Jerusalem is not excluded. The gospel is for the Jews if they accept it, but its nature is universal, so if they cannot accept it. It will be accepted by others who have a legitimate and divine right to the salvation it offers.

🖉 This fine piece of work thoroughly deserves an A grade.

■ ■ ■

C-grade answer to A2 question 3

All the gospels tell the story of the life of Jesus, but each from a slightly different perspective, depending on the author's own purposes. One of the main purposes of the author of Luke, according to scholars, is to show to all people the universal nature of God's love.

🖉 This is a very common way for candidates to approach such questions. Unfortunately, it gains no marks because it doesn't tell us anything, but simply paraphrases the question. Try to avoid this.

Luke's gospel seems to be aimed at the Gentiles, that is non-Jews, and to that extent shows that Luke is trying to tell all people about God's love. One of the most important ways in which Luke does this is through the concept of salvation. Luke suggests that everyone needs to be saved from the power of sin and that this can be done through faith in Jesus. He makes the point that this salvation is open to everyone, not just the Jews. For example, Luke shows Jesus preaching to the Samaritans and to outcasts, and in the Birth Narratives there is the prophecy that Jesus will be 'a light of revelation to the Gentiles' (Luke 2:32). Later on, Jesus commands his disciples to 'preach to all nations' (Luke 24:47).

🖉 These are good examples and the point is well made.

Luke also discusses the extent to which Jesus takes his ministry to social outcasts. Jesus is seen associating with tax collectors such as Zacchaeus and Levi, and he dined with 'sinners', much to the annoyance of the Jewish authorities. Jesus said: 'I have come not to call the righteous, but sinners to repentance' (5:32). Jesus also shows God's love for all people in the parables of the lost son and the great banquet.

🖉 Again, the candidate is on the right lines. However, this paragraph lacks detail — it reads like a 'list' of incidents. There needs to be more detail and discussion of the significance.

Luke also highlights Jesus's ministry towards women, who, according to many scholars, had an inferior status in Jewish society. Jesus allowed women to accompany his group and to listen to his teachings, and he performed miracles for them, such as the incident involving the crippled woman and the widow of Nain. He is anointed by the sinful woman in the house of Simon the Pharisee (Luke 7:36–50) and uses women in parables, such as that of the lost coin and the unjust judge.

Here is the crux of the problem. The candidate has highlighted certain issues regarding the universality of God's love, but the essay is rapidly becoming just a catalogue of events and references without any substantial discussion of the issues raised. Note the vague expression 'many scholars' — candidates must name them for the highest marks.

Finally, Luke highlights Jesus's ministry to the poor. Luke says that Jesus came to preach to the poor and he makes the point that the poor are particularly important in God's kingdom: 'Blessed are you who are poor' (Luke 6:20). Jesus spoke about caring for the poor and warned about the problems of wealth and showed that those who gave away what they had, like Zacchaeus, would be blessed. Indeed, the scholar Marshall said that the teaching of Jesus brought good news to the poor and warnings to the rich. Moreover, in the Magnificat, Mary's song says: 'He has filled the hungry with good things, but has sent the rich away empty' (Luke 1:53).

ⓔ The candidate clearly knows this part of the text and quotes well here, but again the discussion lacks depth. For example, why does God care for the poor? Are the rich not included in God's universal love?

Other scholars have suggested that Luke has a different purpose from highlighting the universality of God's love. For instance, some say that Luke is a kind of history book, coming before Acts (also written by Luke), showing the development of the early Church. Others claim that it is an apologia — a book designed to tell the Romans and others that Jesus was not a criminal and that Christians were not a threat.

ⓔ The candidate has rightly gone on to suggest that the gospel may have different purposes, but then simply jots them down without discussion or explanation.

The gospel also emphasises the Second Coming of Christ, and scholars such as Morris say that this would be a time of joy and salvation for all people who had faith in Jesus. This links in with the views of some scholars on the coming of the kingdom of God; in Luke the matter is confusing — sometimes Jesus says the kingdom of God is near, and at other times it seems to be much later. The scholar Käsemann says that Luke thought that it would be in the distant future.

ⓔ This is a weak paragraph. The themes of the Second Coming and the kingdom of God are touched on, but not developed, and the use of scholars is poor — we need to know why, for instance, Käsemann says what he does.

Although we do not know for certain what Luke's purpose was, we can see that the emphasis he places on the Gentiles, women, the poor and social outcasts, highlights the great importance of God's love for all people.

ⓔ This is a common style of ending when candidates don't know what to say. It is a little bit of padding to round things off and simply repeats the question and the substance of the essay.

The Passion Narratives

Discuss and analyse the religious symbolism contained in the
Crucifixion Narrative of Luke's gospel.

(20 marks)

A-grade answer to A2 question 4

Luke's gospel uses Mark's essential structure for the Passion Narrative, but like Matthew, the Evangelist has included new material, omitted certain Marcan elements, and restructured the narrative to suit his purposes. Frank Matera observes: 'Luke's editorial activity explains most of the differences since this section reflects the theology present in the rest of the gospel.' Hence we find that the religious symbolism of the Passion Narratives reflects many of the themes and images that Luke has already developed earlier in his work.

> A strong answer to this question will only be possible if the candidate avoids lengthy and tedious narrative. All bodes well here, and it appears that the answer will be directed towards the question given rather than to a vague invitation to 'write all you remember of the Crucifixion Narratives'.

From the moment Jesus is led to the cross, Luke continues to maintain his theme of Jesus's innocence. He writes 'as they led him away' and it is clear that 'they' are the Jewish leaders who have persuaded Pilate to condemn Jesus to death. Although Luke knows that Jeus was convicted by a Roman court, he leaves the text ambiguous to heighten the Jewish responsibility. The mourning women who follow Jesus to the place of crucifixion may well be professional mourners, although the sympathy and support of women for Jesus and his ministry is obviously a dominant theme in the gospel. However, the primary point of the story is Jesus's prophecy over Jerusalem. Citing Hosea 10:8 he makes clear that the sins of God's people have reached a climax in their condemnation of Jesus and their punishment will now be as great as that which faced their ancestors in Samaria.

> A decision has to be made as to where the Crucifixion Narrative begins and ends. Luke 22:26–49, or its parallels in the other gospels, is an ideal block of material to work with.

At the cross the narrative follows the Marcan framework, but Luke attributes greater significance to the criminals who hang next to Jesus. He identifies them as 'two others also, who were criminals' to distinguish them from Jesus, who clearly is not a criminal — this has been established by Pilate's and Herod's declarations of his innocence at the trials. Luke may see the fulfilment of Jesus's words from Isaiah 22:37 here — 'and he was reckoned with transgressors'. Jesus, the innocent martyr, speaks forgiveness to his persecutors even as he hangs on the cross, and it is not surprising that some scribes found the words so difficult that they were omitted from some manuscripts. However, it is fitting for Luke that Jesus should face death with forgiveness and reconciliation on his lips, since that has been a primary theme of the gospel (e.g. the Parable of the Lost Son). One of the criminals also recognises Jesus's innocence, contributing to a picture that is systematically constructed throughout the Passion Narrative. His humble acknowledgement — 'We are receiving the due reward of our deeds; but this man has done nothing wrong' — contrasts sharply with the mockery of the bystanders and the Jewish leaders. Appropriately, 'Luke portrays Jesus as the Messiah who refuses to save himself, but continues to save others even at the moment of death' (Matera), and the criminal receives forgiveness and the promise of salvation in his dying hours.

This candidate continues to display a good blend of textual knowledge with scholarly commentary.

Luke adds a distinctive element to the account of Jesus's death. Like Mark, he records the eclipse and the tearing of the temple curtain, but he does not employ the so-called cry of dereliction which is found in Mark and Matthew, but rather at the moment of Jesus's death he prays aloud, 'Father, into your hands I commit my spirit.' Like the cry of dereliction, this is taken from the Psalms (31:5), and by using it here Luke changes the mood utterly. Rather than dying as an abandoned Son of God (or so it may appear), he dies as the 'suffering righteous one who peacefully entrusts his soul to the Father' (Matera), uttering a prayer that Gordon Reid observes 'was commonly used by Jewish mothers as a prayer taught to children before they went to sleep at night'.

The centurion's declaration of Jesus's innocence is more than a legal claim, but rather it contains the notion of righteousness. This indicates that a person is in a right relationship with God, as Elizabeth and Zechariah were described as righteous, law-abiding Jews. Ironically, it is Jesus, not his Jewish persecutors, who stands in a righteous relationship with God, as does the righteous sufferer of the Psalms, which all the Evangelists employ freely in the Passion Narratives. The centurion praises God as he speaks these words, the ninth occasion on which Luke uses this verb to describe those conveying praise at God's saving activity. The centurion, like other characters in the gospel, praises God because he manifests his saving activity in Jesus the Saviour, the innocent martyr and Davidic king, who dies so that all men might be reconciled to God.

The candidate concludes by demonstrating knowledge of the whole gospel in relation to the Crucifixion Narrative. It is characteristic of an A-grade candidate to consider connections rather than learning material in the form of isolated topics.

■ ■ ■

C-grade answer to A2 question 4

Luke's account of the crucifixion contains a number of elements that are unique to him. First, on the way to the cross, Jesus is followed by weeping women. Jesus addresses them as 'Daughters of Jerusalem' and tells them that their mourning for him should be converted to mourning for themselves. It is thought that he is referring to the destruction of Jerusalem which had occurred in 70 CE, but which he is putting as a prophecy into Jesus's mouth. The traumatic event which lies in the future as far as the women are concerned will be so terrifying that even barren women will be envied. This is a remarkable thing to say in a society in which barrenness was considered a curse from God. Jesus goes on to say to the women: 'For if they do this when the wood is green, what will happen when it is dry?' By this he is suggesting that he is the innocent party — the green wood — wrongfully condemned, and if he is treated in such a way, how much worse will it be for those who are guilty?

> e This candidate has started at a good point in the narrative — the road to the cross — and has given an accurate summary of the episode of the weeping women. What remains to be seen is whether the candidate will just continue with a basic narrative approach, with the odd comment here and there, or whether the symbolic and theological significance of the material will be precisely identified.

On the cross Luke puts much more emphasis on the criminals who are crucified with Jesus, and the conversation that Jesus has with them is one of the most famous in Christian literature. First, Jesus forgives those who are crucifying him with the amazing words: 'Father, forgive them, for they do not know what they are doing.' The bystanders mock him, as does one of the criminals, but the other one recognises the significance of Jesus and his innocence. He responds immediately with a promise of salvation for the criminal: 'Truly I say to you, today you will be with me in Paradise.'

> e It appears that the candidate has taken the former approach and concentrated on narrative. Also, by whose standards is the conversation 'one of the most famous in Christian literature' and who decided that Jesus's words are 'amazing'? These are subjective value judgements and have no place in an A-level essay.

As in Mark, there is darkness over the land at the time of Jesus's death, and the curtain in the temple tears in two, signifying that Jesus has broken down the divisions within Judaism and all men can come close to God. Luke adds two more important sayings. First, when Jesus dies he does not cry out 'My God, my God, why have you forsaken me?' but instead he says 'Father, into your hands I commit my spirit'. Luke has chosen to portray Jesus's death as being more peaceful than it was in Mark and Matthew.

> e This is too simplistic an assessment of profound characteristics.

The second difference is that the centurion at the foot of the cross does not say 'Truly this man was the Son of God', but 'This man was innocent/righteous'. Luke has had an interest in the concept of righteousness since the beginning of the gospel (all the characters in the Birth Narrative are righteous Jews) and he is concerned to show that at his death Jesus was recognised by a representative of the Roman authorities as innocent, not a criminal who deserved to die. This is important for Luke's second volume — Acts — which shows how the Church had to survive in a hostile political and religious environment and needed to be able to show that Christianity was not a revolutionary religion.

🄴 This is a good approach to take at the end of the essay, but it's a bit rushed and assumes the reader's prior understanding of the issue. Many opportunities for development have been lost in this essay, making it impossible to raise the grade above a C.

The Prologue to the Fourth Gospel

Discuss and assess the views of scholars concerning the content and the purpose of the Prologue to the Fourth Gospel. (20 marks)

A-grade answer to A2 question 5

The style, purpose and themes of the Prologue have all been carefully dissected by scholars who continue to debate the nature of this profound piece of theological writing. It remains something of an enigma, since there is no consensus as to whether it is an original part of the gospel or a later addition. J. A. T. Robinson argues that it is an addition put in to draw together the themes of the gospel, to offer some kind of closure, as we may argue the Epilogue (chapter 21) also serves to do. Furthermore, we need to consider whether it was a free composition by the Evangelist or his school, or whether he/they drew on an existing poem or hymn. Burney claims that it is an Aramaic hymn, written in a simple poetic style, making frequent use of 'and', a characteristic of Hebrew poetry. He suggests that the Greek translation was not well done, an indication that the Prologue is an Aramaic original.

Note the key word in the question — 'scholars'. It would not be acceptable, therefore, to write out a general list of things in the Prologue without any reference to scholarly debate about them. Fortunately, this candidate is clearly structuring the answer around scholarly contributions.

C. K. Barrett suggests alternatively that the Prologue is distinctively Johannine, adopting a thematic approach, and as such it acts as a curtain-raiser to the gospel. Its style is like that of the Christological hymns adopted by Paul in Philippians 2:6–11 and Colossians 1:15–20, retracing Jesus's heavenly origins, the taking on of flesh, his acceptance of his death, and his exaltation to God's side.

Whether or not the Prologue is a later addition, or a separate hymn employed by the Evangelist or a redactor, it is uncannily accurate in its anticipation of the gospel themes. Graham Stanton speaks of it as a 'lens' through which to see the rest of the gospel, Barrett as a 'porch' through which we enter it, and Morna Hooker as a 'key' which unlocks the gospel's message. She writes: 'In his unique introduction, this Evangelist has given us the key that enables us to understand his Gospel...The Evangelist's opening paragraphs find their fulfilment in Jesus's glorious death.'

This candidate is using scholarship wisely, not trying to pull the wool over the examiner's eyes with silly claims such as 'Barrett says that the Prologue opens with the words "In the beginning"'.

From the beginning of the Prologue the Evangelist makes clear that Jesus's origin is to be traced back to creation itself. He echoes Genesis 1:1 in his opening line: 'In the beginning...,' and allies Jesus, the Word, with God from eternity, not from a stable in Bethlehem. Gospel themes come thick and fast: light and life; conflict ('The light shines in the darkness, and the darkness has not overcome it'); witness; new birth; glory; truth; and — most of all — the vital truth that Jesus is the fullest revelation of God available to man.

The Prologue is constructed in such a way as to suggest that the poetic framework has been interspersed with other material about John the Baptist. Rudolph Bultmann suggests that the purpose of the gospel may well be to demonstrate to followers of John that he was not the Messiah and that they should transfer their allegiance to Jesus. Verses 6–8 and 15 interrupt the flow of the poem and may indeed be later insertions, but we would be hard pressed to suggest that the purpose of the whole gospel could be based on these two references, plus a smattering of others in the first half of the gospel.

@ This candidate supports all the observations made about the text with scholarly material. The answer demonstrates how important it is to have more than one scholar's views at your fingertips if you are to tackle successfully a question of this type.

Bultmann also emphasises the possible Gnostic associations in the gospel that can be detected in the Prologue. The Evangelist writes: 'The true light that enlightens every man was coming into the world...' (John 1:9), suggesting that Jesus is the heavenly redeemer come to earth to ignite the divine spark in all men. Later on there are other possible traces of this theme: Jesus is the one from above who descends to earth; the one who links heaven and earth; the one who brings words of knowledge and wisdom which lead to salvation. But again, Bultmann may be making too much of fairly random and undeveloped points. The Evangelist appears to have an interest in engaging readers from many religious and cultural backgrounds and it is unlikely that he would have been writing for Gnostic thinkers to the exclusion of all others.

Two themes perhaps emerge as more important than others for understanding the relationship of the Prologue: the incarnation of the Logos, and the transcending of Judaism by the gospel. The first of these themes reaches a climax in John 1:14 — 'And the Word became flesh and dwelt among us'. This is the 'scandal' of the Prologue — that the pre-existent divine word can take on mortal flesh and be tabernacled among men. Augustine claimed that he had learnt the substance of the Prologue from Greek philosophy, but that the Word could take on flesh was utterly without precedent. It is, however, what God's people in the Old Testament had been longing for — that God would come down among them for their salvation — 'O that thou wouldst rend the heavens and come down...' (Isaiah 64:1). In Jesus, God does exactly this: 'In the Prologue, the author declares that Jesus Christ is God himself, known in terms of mortal flesh and life' (Gordon Reid).

e The candidate has, rightly, been selective in the latter stages of this essay. It is neither possible nor useful to cover every aspect of the Prologue, so two key areas have been selected for attention.

Morna Hooker identifies the second of these themes as one that is permanently at work in the pages of the gospel. She writes: 'We shall perhaps understand what is going on behind the pages of the Fourth Gospel if we think of it as a gigantic take-over bid. The old, established firm is Judaism. The newcomers are the Christians, and they lay claim to everything within Judaism. But the basis of their claim is...that the original founder of the firm had intended them to take it over....' Hooker sees this unfolding in the Prologue: 'The law was given through Moses; grace and truth came through Jesus Christ' (John 1:17). This is the climax of the Prologue and the beginning of the theme which is constantly played out — at the wedding at Cana, the cleansing of the temple, in the conflict discourses, and ultimately on the cross, when Jesus, the perfect Passover Lamb, dies for the salvation of man, accomplishing a victory that the Law could not achieve.

e This is an excellent answer. It is an ideal example of what top-grade candidates should be looking to achieve in the exam.

■ ■ ■

C-grade answer to A2 question 5

The Prologue to the Fourth Gospel is one of the most impressive pieces of theological writing in the New Testament and one of the hardest to get to grips with. Scholars are therefore divided over many issues concerning it and there is still no universal agreement.

e What a meaningless opening paragraph. It's obvious that this candidate has read somewhere, or been told, that the Prologue is 'impressive', but there is no point in starting the essay with this unsubstantiated assertion.

The first important issue to resolve is whether the Evangelist wrote the Prologue, or whether it is a later addition, or perhaps a poem that was already circulating in the early Church. Robinson claims that it is a later addition intended to 'round things off', while Barrett disagrees and suggests that it is so characteristically like the gospel because of its language and themes. It is impossible to reach an agreement on this because there is no evidence of the Prologue existing or circulating separately, but we do know that there were hymns like this in the early Church. An example is Colossians 1:15–20, which has many similar features to John's Prologue.

e The candidate has read the wording of the question and seen that a discussion of the contribution of scholars is required — so this is promising, although the discussion does not run very deep so far.

Another issue of concern to scholars is what language the Prologue was written in, and Burney and Torrey argue that it was originally an Aramaic text and was later translated into Greek.

[e] This part of the answer is too brief to be of much value.

Marsh claims that the Prologue is intended to pick up and develop the devices that were used in the Synoptics and I think this is a good point. In the Synoptics the writers seem to be more concerned about the historical origin of Jesus. Matthew and Luke have Birth Narratives that show Jesus being born in a human fashion, while Mark starts straight away with Jesus's ministry, with no information at all about his origin. The Prologue goes further than any of these and makes clear that Jesus's origin is heavenly and not earthly. It starts before creation and leads up to a climax that is the Word becoming flesh. The Prologue therefore shows that although Jesus was pre-existent with God, God's plan is fulfilled through the Word coming to earth. Because Jesus is pre-existent, he is fully God, and throughout his ministry he demonstrates this in his signs and his teachings about himself. The Prologue introduces this idea very clearly and could be seen to be a key to the gospel.

[e] Given that the question has instructed the candidate to assess the views of scholars, it would have been good to see another scholar's contribution included in this paragraph. The first sentence of this paragraph contains the dreadful phrase 'I think'. The examiner is not particularly interested in what you think, but rather whether you can objectively value scholarly material.

Scholars have also debated whether John was influenced by Greek philosophy in writing the Prologue. The use of Logos is only found in the Fourth Gospel and it is a very significant term. It is translated as Word, but there are many meanings to it. In the Old Testament it was the word of God, and in Greek philosophy it could be understood as reason or order. It is also possible that there are Gnostic influences in the Prologue as there are in the whole gospel, although not all scholars agree that this is the case.

[e] The rather vague words 'Scholars have also debated…' enable the candidate to avoid naming any particular individual. Since barely two scholars are ever in agreement over a matter of biblical exegesis it really is pretty meaningless.

John the Baptist makes his first appearance in the Prologue and another issue for scholars is whether the Prologue is a polemic against him. A polemic is material that is intended to attack a point of view — in this case, that John was the Messiah.

[e] This is turning into a list of short paragraphs, each making one point but without developing it into a discussion or giving any textual support for it. Perhaps a single mark may be picked up for each point, but there can be little or no credit for evaluation.

Finally, the Prologue ends with the promise that Jesus, who is in the bosom of the Father, will reveal God to man. This is possible because Jesus is God himself and so is the full revelation of God, as Jesus says later to Philip: 'Do you not know that if you have seen me you have seen the Father?'

🄴 What a pity that this candidate has not demonstrated more knowledge of how Prologue themes are developed later in the gospel. This brief allusion to the Farewell Discourses has come too late to gain much credit, since the essay ends rather abruptly with no discussion of the point. This is another example of an essay that could so easily have been developed into a top-grade response but did not take advantage of its own opportunities. Unfortunately, it is typical of the work of many candidates who end up puzzling over why they achieved a grade well below their expectations.

Conflict

Examine the relationship between Jesus and the religious and political authorities as presented in the Fourth Gospel, and assess the reasons why, according to the Fourth Evangelist, Jesus was put to death.

(20 marks)

A-grade answer to A2 question 6

The conflict between Jesus and the religious and political authorities occurs for different reasons, but they nevertheless overlap by the time we reach the final stages of Jesus's ministry. The crucifixion of Jesus is made possible by an association between religious and political figures, although their motivations are somewhat different.

Conflict as a central theme in the Fourth Gospel is established as early as the Prologue: 'The light shines in the darkness, and the darkness has not overcome it' (John 1:5). Although the darkness did not succeed in triumphing over the light, the fact that it attempted to do so is evident throughout the gospel. Smalley observes: 'The contrast between Jesus as light and his enemies — who are also the enemies of God — as darkness is sustained throughout the gospel, particularly in the debates between Jesus and the Jews.'

The candidate has demonstrated an awareness that conflict issues relate to the gospel as a whole and not just the Passion Narrative.

John shows Jesus in conflict with Judaism at the beginning of his public ministry. At the wedding at Cana he has already symbolically demonstrated that he will transcend and transform the old order, but at the cleansing of the temple this is brought into dramatic focus. His outrageous display in the trading area of the temple draws the response 'What sign have you to show us for doing this?'— in other words, 'What is your authority for doing this?' The Jewish authorities are outraged that Jesus can challenge the temple — God's house, and the centre of Jewish life and worship — and that challenge is tantamount to blasphemy.

Jesus continues to challenge the religious authorities in this way. Two Sabbath healings lead to intense Christological debates concerning the authority under which Jesus acts, and Jesus's claim, 'My father is working still, and I am working' (John 5:17), accurately interpreted as a divine claim, leads to concerted action to put Jesus to death. The healing of the blind man, also on a Sabbath, culminates in the excommunication of the man from the synagogue, making clear that the fate of a true Johannine disciple will be no different to that of Jesus.

This is a good, systematic approach, working chronologically through the gospel without falling into narrative.

Even in discourse with the religious authorities the nature of the conflict is made clear. Graham Stanton observes that the Fourth Gospel is both the most Jewish and the most anti-Jewish gospel, and its anti-Semitism is evident in the strongly worded exchanges. Jesus calls the Jewish authorities children of the devil (John 8:44), and not seekers of the truth since they are not of God (8:46–47). They take many opportunities to kill him, but since Jesus's death is firmly under divine control, they do not succeed since 'his hour had not yet come' (8:20).

However, the nature of the conflict with the religious authorities does not simply rest on religious issues. The Sanhedrin was appointed by Rome to monitor the political atmosphere and it was their responsibility to ensure that potential crowd drawers and rebels were not allowed to get out of control. After the raising of Lazarus, Jesus's following has grown to dangerous proportions and the Jewish council must respond. Their observation that 'If we let him go on thus, every one will believe in him and the Romans will come and destroy both our holy place and our nation' reflects a genuine fear. Ellis Rivkin writes of the society in which Jesus preached: 'In such a world, even the most nonpolitical of charismatics took his life in his hand when he preached the good news of God's coming kingdom.' Caiaphas identifies the solution: '…it is expedient that one man should die for the people and that the whole nation should not perish' (John 11:50). The religious and political systems had become intertwined in attempting to retain control and Jesus inevitably became a victim of the system.

Interesting use is made of scholarship and the candidate is able to demonstrate an awareness of the cultural background to the narratives.

Pilate stands as a lone figure in a struggle to protect Jesus from the religious system that wants him dead. As the sole representative of Roman governorship, he is nevertheless sympathetic, clearly identifying that the Jewish authorities have their own axe to grind, but under the restrictions of Roman occupation they cannot take the law into their own hands and execute Jesus themselves. He repeatedly declares Jesus innocent, but finally submits when the Jews utter the strongest threat they can make — a report to Rome that Pilate has not acted in the best interests of the empire (John 19:12). He attempts to redress the balance on the cross with the controversial title 'The King of the Jews'. The religious authorities are offended by the implicit claim that they have allowed their king to be condemned to death, but in a show of boldness, Pilate refuses to change the title.

The Fourth Evangelist clearly suggests that the primary responsibility for Jesus's death lay with the Jewish leaders, and he treats them harshly because of it. However, they were acting within the constraints of their time and their understanding of what was religiously acceptable. Ultimately, of course, Jesus had to die because God had determined that it should be so: 'God so loved the world that he gave his only son, that whoever believes in him should not perish but have eternal life' (John 3:16). Throughout his ministry Jesus alludes frequently to his impending and unavoidable death — '"And I, when I am lifted up from the earth, will draw all men to myself." He said this to show by what death he was to die' (John 12:32–33). He does not avoid it, because he knows that it is the only means by which man is to be reconciled with God. His death is therefore an accomplishment and a victory and although the religious authorities are culpable, they are the instruments with which God has chosen to accomplish the great act of salvation.

ℯ This answer has neatly tied together the religious, political and theological reasons for Jesus's death and is clearly the work of a very skilled student.

■ ■ ■

C-grade answer to A2 question 6

The religious authorities in the Fourth Gospel are presented very negatively by the Evangelist and are always shown as being against Jesus. This may not have been entirely true since the Evangelists may be writing with a bias against them, but in the Fourth Gospel they are used to show the opposition of the Jews against Jesus and he has some very strong scenes of conflict with them. They are usually the Pharisees, although the religious authorities included the Sanhedrin, the priests and the scribes.

Pilate, who is the Roman governor, represents the political authorities. We only encounter him in the trial scenes, but he is presented much more sympathetically than the religious authorities.

ℯ So far, so good. The candidate has made an accurate distinction between religious and political authorities. Now we need to see how this is all specific to the Fourth Gospel.

Jesus came into conflict with the religious authorities over the keeping of the law. The Pharisees were concerned especially about the Sabbath and they had 39 regulations about what couldn't be done on the Sabbath day. These regulations all concerned working, and much of Jesus's conflict with the religious authorities centred around whether he was breaking the Sabbath by working. The Pharisees were the largest of the religious parties and they were very concerned to keep the Law alive and relevant at a time when Palestine was occupied by Gentile forces. They kept themselves apart from the ordinary people and are presented in the gospels as being very critical of those who did not keep the Law as strictly as they did. They built a hedge around the Law so that there was no danger of them accidentally breaking a law. They are often condemned as hypocrites with no love and compassion for people who were not as obedient as they were, but this may be an unfair picture, since they were genuinely concerned with keeping the Law alive when it could easily have been lost.

ℯ There is a lack of direction here. All this information is perfectly valid and interesting, but it is outside the scope of the present question. If the candidate continues like this, time will run out and the opportunity to gain enough marks for a strong grade will be lost.

Jesus has two major conflicts with the religious authorities about keeping the Sabbath. The first is when he heals the lame man at the pool. He tells the man to pick up his mat and to walk, which he does, but carrying a burden from one place to another is forbidden on the Sabbath and the Pharisees question him about it. He says that Jesus told him to do it, putting the blame onto Jesus. When Jesus finds the man in the temple, the man seems to have no interest in learning anything more about Jesus, so he is something of a failure as a disciple. The Pharisees challenge Jesus about why he told the man to carry the mat and Jesus gives the startling answer: 'My Father is working still and I am working.' The Pharisees understand this as blasphemy and it is the reason that they set out to kill him. Jesus has not only broken the Sabbath but has called God his own father and so they have two reasons now to condemn him. J. L. Martyn suggests that this is the reason that the Jews persecuted the Johannine community. They worshipped Jesus as God, which was blasphemous, and this led to their separation from Judaism.

e This answer shows that a lot has been learned, but the question is not being targeted precisely, so much of the effort is wasted.

In the second Sabbath healing, Jesus makes mud, which he puts on the blind man's eyes. Mixing dust and spittle was also seen as working, because a new substance was created. The blind man, however, is far more positive about what happens than the lame man had been, and when he is tackled about what Jesus did he supports Jesus and is ultimately prepared to be excommunicated for it. The Pharisees seem to suspect that something has happened that shows them in a bad light, for they say to Jesus: 'Are we blind too?' but they do not repent.

Some Pharisees clearly did support Jesus, and Nicodemus is the primary example of this. Early in the gospel he comes to Jesus at night and does not seem to understand his teachings, but by the end of the gospel it is possible that he is a disciple, although he might be a 'crypto-Christian' — someone who believes in Jesus but does not openly confess it.

e This is an interesting point but we seem to be quite a long way from assessing the reasons why Jesus was put to death.

After Jesus raises Lazarus from the dead the Jewish authorities make a concerted effort to arrest him and he is eventually brought before Pilate. The religious authorities do not really have any good reason to put Jesus to death and Pilate seems to know this, because he asks them 'What charge have you against this man?' and they can only give a very general reply. Pilate also seems to be quite sympathetic towards Jesus and asks him who he is and where he is from, and 'What is truth?' However, Pilate is not able to stand up against the Jewish crowds, which are determined to see Jesus condemned. They threaten Pilate by saying 'If you release this man you are not Caesar's friend' and so Pilate has no choice but to go along with what they want if he is not to be reported to Rome as an unsuitable governor.

> ⓔ We could do with some consideration here of why the religious authorities were compelled to go to Pilate to get the death penalty. Why not just kill Jesus themselves?

The reasons why Jesus was put to death are quite complex, but essentially it was because he alienated himself from the religious authorities and because Pilate was too weak to stand up for him at the trial. If Pilate had been able to stand by his conviction that Jesus did not deserve to die, then the story would have been a very different one.

> ⓔ It certainly would! But this is a rather naïve concluding statement. The candidate doesn't seem to have any idea that Jesus had to die to fulfil God's plan of salvation. As far as the Evangelist is concerned, no different story is possible. With more guidance this candidate could have produced a much better answer, focusing on the question and applying stricter tests of relevance to the material used rather than pouring out an endless and somewhat unselective flow of information.

Early Church matters: the Letter to the Corinthians

(a) Explain Paul's teachings in 1 Corinthians on marriage and worship. (14 marks)

(b) Evaluate the importance of these teachings for the early Church. (6 marks)

A-grade answer to A2 question 7

(a) Paul's letter to the Corinthians clearly addresses issues that the Church was finding difficult to assess, and his replies attempt to place them within the perspective of an eschatological community, the pagan origins of which have ill prepared its members for the challenges of living a gospel-centred life.

> 🄴 A sign of a good candidate is the ability to place issues and texts within their relevant contemporary setting, as has been done here.

Paul's teaching concerning marriage addresses both the single and the married. His conviction is that it is better to remain unmarried, and this primarily derives from the time in which Paul wrote. For a community actively anticipating the end times, the best state in which to be is one that enables the believer to focus on their commitment to God, unhindered by the concerns of a marriage partner. F. F. Bruce observes: 'The pressures of the remaining interval (until the parousia) will be such that the man or woman of faith must accept the discipline of iron rations and be as free as possible from the ordinary and legitimate distractions of secular life.'

> 🄴 Early use of relevant scholarship bodes well.

However, Paul is aware that the ability to accept singleness with equanimity is a divine gift: 'I wish that all were as I myself am. But each has his own special gift from God, one of one kind and one of another' (1 Corinthians 7:7). Therefore, he must make provision for those for whom singleness is not possible. Paul cannot dismiss marriage for most members of his church, but he does propose guidelines. Since he believes that the purpose of marriage is to provide an outlet for human sexuality, if a man and woman feel compelled to marry, then neither partner should refuse the other sexual relations. Celibacy is a vocation, and to enforce it on a marriage partner misses the whole point of choosing marriage rather than celibacy.

Furthermore, Paul advocates that once married, a couple should remain united, although he makes a concession — the so-called Pauline Privilege — for those who are married to unbelievers. A non-Christian partner is not under condemnation should the unbelieving spouse feel unable to continue in the marriage. Again, this should be understood within the context of Paul's time, since many new converts may have faced matrimonial difficulties if their partners were not also converted. Potentially, the believing partner is the means of sanctification for the non-believer and their children, but there is no obligation upon the believer to remain 'bound' to a marriage the non-believer no longer wants. Bruce suggests that Paul may have been speaking from personal experience here.

🄴 This is a bit of an off-the-cuff scholarly observation which in this case is not especially valuable — it is, however, typical of the way many candidates use it.

Paul's primary concern is that a Christian should not be eager to change the state in which he or she was called: 'Concern to change one's status could absorb energies which might be more profitably devoted to Christian life and service' (Bruce). This applies not only to marriage but also to social status, but marriage involves a commitment to another person, and Paul would rather that a Christian should be unconcerned by such a commitment when preparing for the parousia.

As far as worship is concerned, Paul addresses issues of order and the edification of the Church. Worship in Corinth — and presumably in the other New Testament churches — was charismatic, and Paul's concern is to ensure that the spiritual freedom of worship should not undermine its purpose. The most outwardly glamorous gift as far as the Corinthians were concerned appears to have been *glossolalia*. Whilst Paul acknowledged that he speaks in tongues more than anyone, he is concerned that this gift should not be misused. Tongues has far less potential than prophecy for benefiting others — 'He who speaks in a tongue edifies himself, but he who prophesies edifies the church' (1 Corinthians 14:4) — and so prophecy should be valued more highly as a means of building up the faith and worship life of the whole Church community.

🄴 Throughout the essay the candidate has been using the text with fluency and skill, and this continues here.

Worship should also have missionary power and this is impossible if potential converts hear tongues. These will naturally be incomprehensible to them and will give them no reason to believe in the gospel, as 'Its incommunicability, not its irrationality, makes its presence inappropriate in the gatherings of the community' (Robert Banks). Tongues must therefore be accompanied by interpretation if they are to have meaning.

Worship should then be characterised by an orderly structure: only one person speaks at a time, prophecy should be weighed, tongues interpreted, and the 'spirits of the prophets subject to the prophets'. Paul concludes that in worship, 'All things should be done decently and in order' (1 Corinthians 14:40).

(b) These teachings are of course only to be understood fully if seen against the background of the early Church. Paul was writing to a community that was new and was establishing itself in pagan society. Christian ways of life and worship were new to them, and they did not have the tradition of a Jewish background and knowledge of the Old Testament on which to build. Sexual freedom in Corinth was a way of life and Paul's teachings on marriage may have appeared particularly strict and formal, but Paul is concerned to establish for the Corinthians a way of life that will be a powerful witness to non-believers and will equip them for the return of Jesus.

> 🅔 This part of the question really is the sting in the tail. However, it has not floored this candidate, who has a firm grasp of the background to the letters.

Tongues were likely to be given an especially high value in Corinthian society. Hellenistic culture valued wisdom, and tongues would appear mysterious and laden with implications of special knowledge, or gnosis. Earlier in the letter Paul has already declared that: 'For since, in the wisdom of God, the world did not know God through wisdom, it pleased God through the folly of what we preach to save those who believe' (1 Corinthians 1:21). It is not in the interests of the Church, therefore, to encourage the predominance of a gift that could be misinterpreted as purveying a special quality of 'wisdom'. Finally, in a cosmopolitan, pagan community, where a diversity of religious beliefs were spread far and wide, Paul needs to establish solid foundations for the gospel, and in order to do so he must eliminate potential false teachings and heresies at their roots.

> 🅔 A highly competent response, which is easily worthy of an A grade.

■ ■ ■

C-grade answer to A2 question 7

(a) In his letter to the Corinthians, Paul addresses many problems that the Church is having, and two of these are marriage and worship. Paul starts his teaching on marriage with the statement, 'Now concerning the matters about which you wrote', which suggests that the Corinthians had asked him specifically about marriage and how it fitted in with their new life as Christians.

Paul believes that marriage is not the best option for a Christian. He suggests that he is unmarried and that he thinks that to be unmarried is the best way to prepare for Jesus's return. However, he also says: 'It is better to marry than to burn with desire.' In other words, he is saying that if you cannot control your sexual desires then it is better to get married. Paul was celibate but he says that this is a gift from God and not everyone could live that way.

> 🅔 All pretty straightforward so far. More depth will be needed to gain a high grade, however.

Paul goes into some detail about what to do if you are a Christian married to a non-Christian. This would have been relevant to many new Christians in the Corinthian church, since not everyone's partner would have been converted when they were. Paul teaches that the new believer should not set out to separate from the non-believer, but he does recognise that the non-believer might choose not to stay with their newly converted partner. If this is the case, he says the believer is 'not bound'. This means that he or she is free to move on and even to marry again, although in every other case Paul implies that marriage partners should seek to remain together. If they do separate for any other reason, they should not remarry but, if possible, be reconciled to each other.

Even though Paul says that a believer is not under an obligation to stay with a non-believing partner who wants to leave, he does suggest that if they do stay together the non-believing partner may well become a Christian through the influence of the believer. 'Wife, how do you know whether you will save your husband? Husband, how do you know whether you will save your wife?'

e The candidate has continued along the same lines since the beginning of the essay. There is competent and accurate accounting of the factual details of the narrative, but so far we haven't really learned anything about the value of the material.

Ultimately, Paul wants Christians to be free from things that will distract them from their Christian life and from waiting for Jesus to return. He tells the Corinthians that the best thing they can do is to remain in the state they were in when they first believed. If they were single, they should remain single and, if married, remain married.

Worship was also an important issue for the Corinthians. Worship in the Corinthian church was dominated by spiritual gifts such as tongues, and Paul has to write to the Corinthians about the importance of keeping order in the Church. Tongues may be exciting and impressive but they do not help other people, especially people who do not understand what they are about. Paul encourages the Church to value prophecy more highly than tongues. He teaches them that during worship everything should happen in an orderly fashion and they should wait for tongues to be interpreted.

e More explanation about the nature of these gifts and the place they had in worship would have been valuable.

Paul also writes about the Lord's Supper. In the Corinthian church it seems that they were not carrying this out in an orderly fashion either and that some people went hungry while others had too much to eat. Paul tells them to eat at home first so that the meal is one that genuinely commemorates Jesus's death and is not just an excuse for a party.

e I have reservations about whether it is legitimate to include any discussion about the Lord's Supper here. In the Corinthian church it was a fellowship meal rather than the act of worship we more commonly know it as today, and it is more likely to be the subject of a different question altogether.

Paul writes about love in chapter 13 as the basis on which all worship should be established. He says: 'If I speak with the tongues of angels, but have not love, I am nothing.' Worship outside the context of love, therefore, is meaningless.

🅔 This could have been developed into a more interesting and detailed ending.

(b) The early Church faced many difficulties, including persecution, but it also had to adjust to a new faith which called for a way of life that was very different from the old lifestyles. The Corinthians probably found this harder than any of Paul's other churches. Not only were they Gentiles, and so had no Jewish background on which to build, but also Corinth was known to be a place of moral laxity. People came to Corinth from all over the world and there were many pagan religious influences. Paul has to address all kinds of domestic and religious situations that the Corinthians were facing unprepared.

The Corinthians were lovers of wisdom, and the glamorous gift of tongues would have been very attractive to them. Paul has to make them understand that there are more useful gifts for the life of the Church and what is outwardly attractive is not necessarily what is most valuable.

🅔 This is a typical mid-grade response to a knotty question. There is nothing essentially wrong with it, because it is difficult for an A-level candidate to come to any clear conclusions about what a religious community 2,000 years ago *really* thought or did. We can only extrapolate from what knowledge we *do* have. The candidate has introduced some potentially valid points, however, which could certainly have been developed further.

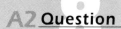

Salvation and eternal life

> **(a)** Examine and analyse the teaching of Jesus on the nature of salvation and eternal life in (i) the conversation with Nicodemus and (ii) the raising of Lazarus. (14 marks)
>
> **(b)** Assess the importance of these teachings for the original readers. (6 marks)

A-grade answer to A2 question 8

(a) The twin concepts of salvation and eternal life have great prominence in the Fourth Gospel. In a sense, they are one and the same thing — if a believer receives salvation, then he or she has eternal life. The word 'salvation' comes from the Greek verb *sozo* meaning 'to make safe or well', and the Fourth Gospel alludes to the notion that people need to be 'saved' from the power of sin, because sin separates humanity from God and this, in turn, means death. Through the saving power of Jesus on the cross, the relationship is restored, death is defeated and the believer has eternal life.

> This is a powerful opening paragraph and shows a clear awareness of the issues and familiarity with the terminology involved.

(i) Although salvation is available to all people, not all will actually be saved, for people will have to choose for themselves whether or not to accept it. This is clear in the conversation between Jesus and Nicodemus. Just prior to the conversation, Jesus cleansed the Temple Market. He did so, according to Marsh, because he was angered by the fact that the Jews had not listened to God's message through the prophets concerning sacrifices and had continued to believe that buying animals and killing them could somehow atone for their sins. His message was that salvation and eternal life would not come from the sacrifice of animals — something different was needed. Enter Nicodemus, a Pharisee and member of the ruling council. His conversation with Jesus highlights the struggle between traditional Judaism and the way of Christ. He comes to Jesus by night, perhaps symbolising the darkness in which he lives, and acknowledges Jesus as a teacher sent from God. But he flounders badly when Jesus tells him: 'No-one can see the kingdom of God unless he is born again' (John 3:3).

> Although lengthy, this paragraph highlights the major points clearly.

Nicodemus has a great knowledge of the Law of Moses, but such knowledge will not bring salvation. He needs to have a personal relationship with God, and to do this he must be born again. Nicodemus does not understand, and this, says Smalley, highlights the shortcomings of Judaism — he can see God's power, but cannot have a personal relationship which comes through being born again, as Ezekiel 37 anticipated. He complains that he cannot re-enter his mother's womb, but this misses the point altogether, prompting Jesus to reply: 'No-one can enter the kingdom of God unless he is born of water and the spirit' (John 3:5).

What Jesus means is that Jewish rituals will not lead to salvation — spiritual rebirth is necessary. Jesus then uses Old Testament imagery, linking the lifting of the serpent by Moses with the lifting of the Son of Man on the cross. In this way, all who believe in him and accept his sacrifice will have salvation and eternal life.

🄴 This is a high-level response with good use of textual narrative, Old Testament symbolism and scholarship.

(ii) The raising of Lazarus is, perhaps, the ultimate symbol of salvation and eternal life. It is an incident that Marsh sees as the crux of the gospel — Lazarus dies as a member of the old Israel and is raised through belief in Christ. For Marsh, the action points forward to the resurrection of Jesus and the bringing of his people out from death to eternal life.

🄴 A good introduction and use of scholarship. This sets the scene well.

Lazarus has been dead and buried for 4 days. Martha, Lazarus's sister, believes that Jesus can still do something and her faith makes her bold enough to say: 'But I know that even now God will give you whatever you ask' (John 11:22). Jesus's response is the famous 'I am' saying: 'I am the Resurrection and the life. He that believes in me will live, even though he dies, and whoever lives and believes in me will never die' (John 11:25).

He is suggesting that the real resurrection will not take place in the distant future, but that the resurrection will take place for believers in and through Jesus — in the present, because all who believe will never die (although it must be noted that Jesus is talking about spiritual rather than physical death). Lazarus is raised from the dead by hearing the voice of Christ, fulfilling an earlier prophecy that Jesus had made: 'The dead will hear the voice of the Son of God and those who hear will live' (John 5:25).

This event, perhaps more than any other, angered the Jewish authorities and led to Jesus's crucifixion. As Tasker points out: 'It was his claim to bestow upon believers the gift of eternal life by raising them from spiritual death which led to his crucifixion.'

🄴 The candidate displays an effective combination of textual knowledge and scholarly analysis.

(b) The teaching of Jesus on salvation and eternal life was crucial to the original readers of the gospel. For believers, it was important as a source of hope, particularly in the dark times of Roman and Jewish persecution, when believers were facing imprisonment, torture and even death for their faith. The promise of salvation and eternal life enabled the early Church to survive.

Jewish readers too would identify with Martha's claim — 'I know he will rise again at the resurrection at the last day', which represents the Pharisaic doctrine of resurrection. Jesus gives it a new significance, however, by rephrasing it in terms of resurrection in the present — a spiritual life which is gained through belief in Jesus in the here and now. This is known as realised eschatology.

e A reasonable point is made clearly, although more detail would help.

The teaching was equally important for non-believers, particularly those well versed in the philosophies of Gnosticism and Stoicism, who might see in Jesus's teaching the fruition of the concepts of the Logos, the holy and eternal world of the spirit, and the corrupt and perishable world of the flesh and salvation through the following of the 'divine light'. It really was a message for all the people.

e An interesting ending, which only the best candidates would have considered. This is a safe A grade.

■ ■ ■

C-grade answer to A2 question 8

(a) Salvation and eternal life are very important themes in the Fourth Gospel. Salvation, which comes from the Greek term 'to make safe or well', is used by Jesus to mean that people must be 'saved' from the power of sin, because sin leads to death. Salvation therefore leads directly to eternal life.

e A competent opening, explaining the key terms.

(i) The conversation with Nicodemus happens soon after Jesus has raided the Temple Market. He did this, much to the anger of the Jewish authorities, because the people were still carrying out the practice of buying and sacrificing animals to God in the hope that he would forgive them their sins. They knew that this was not the case, because the prophets had said so in the Old Testament. Jesus told them that such sacrifices were not the way to salvation and that something different was needed. Soon after, Nicodemus, a leading Pharisee, comes to see him at night, which is, according to the scholar Marsh, symbolic of the darkness he lives in. Jesus tells Nicodemus that he must be 'born again' (John 3:3) and Nicodemus cannot understand. The reason is that Nicodemus knows and understands the Jewish law, but cannot see that it will not lead to eternal life. Jesus tells him that he must start again and develop a new and personal relationship with God. Nicodemus is lost, and complains that he cannot go back into his mother's womb. Jesus then says: 'No-one can see the kingdom of God unless he is born of water and the spirit' (John 3:5).

In fact, what Jesus is saying is that Jewish laws and rituals are not sufficient — a person must be spiritually reborn if they are to be saved. Moreover, spiritual rebirth is only offered to those who believe in Christ.

ⓔ This is rather generalised. It is largely textual, but leaves out some important factors, such as the Old Testament symbolism.

(ii) Marsh says that the raising of Lazarus highlights the death of the old way of things and the birth of the new. It shows that Jesus can bring people from a state of death into life — particularly a state of spiritual death into spiritual life.

ⓔ This is a little vague, but it is nevertheless an interesting beginning with good use of scholarship.

Lazarus has been dead for 4 days before Jesus arrives, but his sister Martha still believes that Jesus can do something. Jesus replies with the famous words: 'I am the resurrection and the life. He that believes in me will live, even though he dies, and whoever lives and believes in me will never die' (John 11:25).

Jesus is saying that salvation is not in the distant future, it is present now, through him, and that all who believe in him will never die. He calls out, and Lazarus is restored to life, just as Jesus predicted: 'The dead will hear the voice of the Son of God and those who hear will live' (John 5:25).

ⓔ The textual narrative is correct, but there is insufficient discussion of the meaning, particularly the notion of spiritual rebirth.

(b) The teaching of Jesus on salvation and eternal life would have been very significant for the original readers of the gospel because they were probably living in a time of great danger, when believers were being persecuted by the Romans and the Jewish authorities and many were facing imprisonment and death. The belief that they would be saved and have eternal life would have given them the strength to endure this ordeal and would enable the early Church to survive and grow.

ⓔ This is a common answer. It is exceedingly brief, and assumes that the only original readers would be members of the early Church. There were others who may have read the gospel, such as educated Greeks and Romans, who may have been influenced in different ways. Overall, this answer will yield a mid-range C grade.

Synoptic question

The new specifications for all boards require candidates to complete a synoptic unit either as coursework or under exam conditions. The principle behind this is that students of religious studies should be able to identify and critically evaluate the links between different parts of their specification. The potential range of combinations is enormous: New Testament/Old Testament and world religions; New Testament/Old Testament and ethics; New Testament/Old Testament and church history; New Testament and Old Testament; New Testament and philosophy. The last essay in this book is a sample synoptic question — with just one A-grade answer — on a popular combination, philosophy of religion and New Testament. Even if this is not the particular combination that you will be taking, read it carefully and take note of the comments made about its features. It is written as if under exam conditions. As such, it is not a piece of coursework that would be subject to certain scholarly conventions such as footnoting.

Synoptic questions demand that you are able to examine a topic — in this case, miracles — from the perspective of two disciplines within your subject. This question demands that the candidate demonstrates knowledge of biblical material and its interpretation, along with philosophical definition of miracles and issues about the nature of God and his action in the world. Too much emphasis on either the New Testament or philosophy will unbalance the essay. It is up to you to work on identifying the links between the approaches and to think laterally about the topic under discussion.

If you are completing a synoptic question under timed exam conditions, you must practise before the examination. Although the titles will vary from year to year, the principles of the question and the links between the disciplines remain the same. You should therefore not have any nasty surprises if you have prepared diligently.

Philosophy and New Testament

'The accounts of miracle stories in the New Testament support a belief in a God who can perform logically impossible actions.' Discuss.   (50 marks)

A-grade answer to A2 question 9

The logically impossible is something that is not only outside our experience, but which logic, reason and the nature of the universe tell us cannot occur. It defies logic that the Red Sea should part, that the sun should reverse its course, or that the dead should be

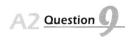

raised. We know that water does not turn into wine, that missing limbs do not regrow, and that the paralysed might conceivably walk again only if they have undergone long, expensive and intensive therapy. Nevertheless, not only the Bible, but also a wealth of Christian testimony handed down over the centuries and in the present day, suggest otherwise. Bible-believing Christians, and those who have experienced miracles in their lives and in the lives of others, claim not only that God does perform miracles but also that the kind of miracle described above may be an infrequent occurrence, but is not logically impossible.

> **e** The introduction has immediately made connections between both disciplines with some consideration of the phrase 'logically impossible' (philosophy) and the kind of biblical miracles that may be considered useful in answering this question (New Testament).

Strictly speaking, therefore, the logically impossible is that which is not merely unexpected or unusual, but that which is inconceivable. It is inconceivable that God could make a square circle, for this would defy the boundaries of logic and reasoning. It is inconceivable that God should commit suicide, or even, perhaps, that he could make a stone too heavy for him to lift (should God engage in such activities). But it is not inconceivable that God should raise the dead, for the whole world order as we know it would not fall apart if he did. While experience tells us that the dead, once dead, remain so, is it actually logically impossible that the dead should rise? Is it utterly inconceivable that a blind man see again, or even for the first time, or that a woman who has suffered years of chronic back pain be instantly cured?

> **e** The candidate is leaving us in no doubt that he or she has understood that a consideration of what would constitute the 'logically impossible' is essential for this answer. A good philosophical awareness is demonstrated in so doing.

The New Testament is full of such accounts. Although miracles are clearly not presented as the reason why men and women should put their faith in Jesus, they were an intrinsic part of his ministry. Miracles confirmed belief — 'This, the first of his signs, Jesus did at Cana in Galilee, and manifested his glory, and his disciples believed in him' (John 2:11); they demonstrated Jesus's authority — 'What is this? With authority he commands even the unclean spirits and they obey him' (Mark 1:27); and they identified him as the Son of God — 'And when they got into the boat, the wind ceased, and those in the boat worshipped him, saying, "Truly you are the Son of God"' (Matthew 14:32–33). Such events were greeted with amazement, wonder and awe; they were evidently beyond the experience of those who witnessed them, who demanded an explanation for them or who were further convinced of what they had already believed about Jesus as a result of listening to his teaching. Jesus performed deeds through the divine power working in him which were at least beyond regular experience, and at most were violations of a natural law: 'transgressions of a law of nature, by the volition of the deity, or by the interposition of some invisible agent' (David Hume's classic definition of miracle).

ⓔ Now the candidate has demonstrated excellent biblical textual knowledge, while still concluding the paragraph with a definition of miracle from an important philosopher.

Aquinas proposed three categories of miracle: first, those acts done by God that nature cannot do. When Jesus raised Lazarus, Jairus's daughter, or the widow of Nain's son, or when Paul brought the unfortunate Eutychus back to life, they were surely doing that which nature cannot do. If these characters were actually dead, then we know that since death is an irreversible state, they could not have been restored to life without the direct power and agency of God. Aquinas's second category of miracles is of things 'done by God that nature could do, but not in this order'. Such miracles might include the healing of the paralysed man. Indeed, many of Jesus's miracles fall into this category: acts that we could conceive of happening within the course of nature, but which experience generally tells us do not occur. However, they are not logically impossible. Where all treatments have failed and the cancer patient is sent home to accept an inevitable death sentence, no one might expect their recovery. But there would be no breach of natural law or logical impossibility if they nevertheless, unexpectedly, and contrary to previous experience drawn from similar cases, went into remission. In such cases, although we might claim that there was no obvious explanation for the recovery, we might equally claim that the simplest explanation was that God intervened miraculously. The official's son (John 4:46–54), the woman who had suffered 12 years of internal bleeding (Luke 8:43–48 &//s) and the leper (Matthew 8:1–4 &//s) enjoyed such healings, which were not logically impossible but were certainly beyond what they expected of nature.

The third category of miracles that Aquinas considered were those things done by God that nature could do, but without the workings of nature. When Jesus cured Peter's mother-in-law of a fever (Mark 1:29–31) there was no suggestion that she was on her deathbed. She presumably had been suffering from something akin to a severe cold or flu, and would have recovered naturally in due course, but Jesus's action expedited the process. Many Christians may believe that God regularly answers their prayers in such a way, so that they may indeed not even consider such events especially miraculous (in the strongest sense of the term), but rather loving responses by God to the prayers of his people.

ⓔ An excellent example of good synoptic practice here, interweaving philosophy (Aquinas's definitions) with New Testament material.

In the New Testament, therefore, Jesus and others (Paul, Peter and John, the 72 sent out by Jesus) perform miracles that fall into all these categories — not only the logically impossible, but events that may warrant the designation miracle but that involve no direct breach of natural law, or violation of logic and reason.

ⓔ Having established a very clear line of argument about the nature of miracle in the New Testament and philosophical definitions of miracles, the candidate now begins the all-important evaluation.

However, it is important to consider the reliability of the New Testament accounts before we conclude that they accurately relate instances of the logically impossible. If, for our purposes, we define a logically impossible event as one that violates a law of nature, we must consider whether the law of nature actually has been broken, whether there was a law of nature at work in the first place (in order for it to be broken), and whether the incident has been correctly understood by those who witnessed it or recorded it.

> 🄔 As in all good exam essays, use of scholarship should be discerning and relevant. In a synoptic essay which is — in theory — twice as long as a regular exam essay, the student should perhaps be looking to include five or six scholarly views, definitions or quotations.

R. H. Fuller argues that we should be wary of claiming that the New Testament miracles are violations of a natural law, since the biblical writers had no concept of natural law as we have today. To them, events were unusual, significant or important, but the evangelists themselves made no claims that Jesus broke natural laws. They did claim that his actions were sufficiently significant to lead observers to evaluate him as possessing divine power, even to be equal to God, but claims that natural laws were violated are left to later interpreters to make.

> 🄔 Here and in the next paragraph the philosophical and biblical material continues to be impressively interwoven, demonstrating that the candidate has an understanding of both, and of the all-important connections between them.

Furthermore, what we may read at one level as biblical accounts of violations of natural law may be explained quite easily in other ways. Rudolph Bultmann famously wrote: 'It is impossible to use electric light and the wireless and to avail ourselves of modern medical and surgical discoveries and, at the same time, to believe in the New Testament world of demons and spirits.' In other words, biblical accounts of miracles owe their origin to an age when the world-view was significantly different from that of our own scientific, rational age. The biblical writers may well have attributed recovery of the Gerasene Demoniac to the casting out of demons, but modern psychiatry might identify him as a victim of multiple personality disorder, calmed and soothed by the presence of Jesus. In a sense, we no longer need (although we may choose) to explain phenomena in terms of the spirit world, and this gives rise to the question of whether the biblical writers were accurate in their assessment of events. Did the Red Sea part through a miraculous act of God, or did a freak wind blow back the waters at the precise moment that the Israelites were pondering how to circumvent this watery obstacle, an event so fortuitous and 'stupendous as to be ever impressed on her memory' (John Bright)?

> 🄔 This paragraph offers more evaluation from both perspectives.

Such interpretations do not necessarily eliminate God from the equation, but they force us to reconsider our understanding of what occurred. God's hand, or that of Jesus, may still be at work in an event that goes utterly against our expectations and that blesses the recipient in ways that had seemed otherwise impossible, but this need not demand that the natural law be broken or that logical impossibilities are achieved. God may work within rather than outside the natural order, bringing to pass things that may happen naturally, but at such times and places when he can breach the epistemic distance and make himself and his nature directly evident to his people. Richard Swinburne suggests: 'If there is a God, one might well expect him to make his presence known to men, not merely through the overall pattern of the universe in which he placed them, but by dealing more intimately and personally with them.' It is not necessary that God do the logically impossible in order to interact with his people in this way, although if he is omnipotent there are strong reasons for believers to maintain that sometimes he will do so.

If the New Testament does support a belief that God can do the logically impossible, there must still be good reasons for him to do so, and a God who acts arbitrarily, or appears to violate the natural order of things without there being obvious benefits for his people, is not a God worthy of worship. If squaring the circle or creating a married bachelor is a truly logically impossible act, then can God perform such a deed? More to the point, should he? If God is omnipotent then presumably he can; if God creates the laws of nature they are within his control, and so too are the laws of logic, mathematics and analytic reasoning. He could change them at will, and declare the triangle a circle, or the queen a king. However, what purpose would be achieved by his so doing? The New Testament does not support such a portrait of God, since all the miracles performed by Jesus or the apostles have a clear purpose: to demonstrate the glory of God. God's glory would not be enhanced by geometric tricks or language games like those of the logical positivists! Not surprisingly, therefore, the New Testament writers, while supporting (within their understanding of such phenomena) a God who may bring men and women back from the dead, and calm the sea with an authoritative word, do not propose a God who arbitrarily changes the principles and laws which hold the universe in place.

📖 The essay concludes with a paragraph that is characterised — as the whole piece has been — with a smooth interweaving of philosophical evaluation and biblical knowledge. This is a very high-level answer indeed.